Foundations and Higher Education:
Dollars, Donors, and Scholars

FOUNDATIONS AND HIGHER EDUCATION:
DOLLARS, DONORS, AND SCHOLARS

In the words of foundation donors,
trustees, and staff . . . Their decisions, accessibility,
grantmaking principles and changing partnership
with higher education

by
Dennis P. McIlnay, Ed.D.

GEORGE KURIAN BOOKS • BOX 519 • BALDWIN PLACE, NY 10505

Library of Congress Cataloging-in-Publication Data

McIlnay, Dennis P., 1948–
    Foundations and higher education : dollars, donors, and scholars /
Dennis P. McIlnay.
        p.   cm.
    Includes bibliographical references and index.
    ISBN 0–914746–28–6 : $29.50
    1. Endowments—United States.   2. Educational fund raising—United
States.   3. Education, Higher—United States—Finance.   I. Title.
LB2336.M36   1991
378'.02'0973—dc20   91–10814
                                                                         CIP

Dedication

To my mother and father,
Katherine and Paul McIlnay

And to my wife, Kathy, with love.

TABLE OF CONTENTS

Tables

ACKNOWLEDGEMENTS

Many people contributed to this book, and I am grateful to them all. Early mentors Sebastian Martorana and Bill Toombs, retired professors at The Pennsylvania State University, taught me how little I knew of American higher education. Jim Gallagher, President of Philadelphia College of Textiles and Science and a long-time friend, encouraged me to study foundations and higher education.

At Seton Hall University, Chuck Dees, Vice Chancellor for University Affairs, was supportive of my doctoral work, as were other colleagues there, especially Phyllis Dunlop, Craig Leach, and Michael McGraw. Marty Finkelstein, Associate Professor of Higher Education at Seton Hall, provided unfailing wisdom as chair of my dissertation committee. John Callan, Dean Emeritus of the College of Education at Seton Hall; Kathleen Rice, Vice President of the Pratt Institute; and Joe Stetar, Associate Provost at Seton Hall, read the study as members of the dissertation committee.

Bob Moore, a friend of many talents, read several chapters of the manuscript, contributing his good humor and great insight.

At Saint Francis College, I must thank many colleagues, especially Randy Frye, Chair of the Business Department; Tom Maher, Vice President for Academic Affairs; Jim McConnell, Professor of Accounting; and Ed Wagner, Professor of Management.

George Kurian, Publisher and Editor, displayed constant enthusiasm for the book.

I am also grateful to family and friends, whose kidding request, "Do we get free copies?", often accompanied their sincere expressions of interest in the book.

I am especially grateful to my parents, who have contributed immensely to my education since Saint Vincent Preparatory School. And though formal education offers many lessons, my best education has been the lesson of their life of good example.

Lastly, I am grateful to my wife, Kathy, who shared every joy and bore every frustration of this project. She participated in endless discussions and read every version of the manuscript. Her contributions to the book are countless, but it is her devotion which I most cherish. Her love has been my best inspiration.

Dennis P. McIlnay
Hollidaysburg, Pennsylvania
January 1990

INTRODUCTION

Foundations are among the nation's most important, but least understood organizations. There are about 25,000 foundations in the United States, but most people would recognize only the largest, the Ford Foundation, or perhaps the most familiar, the Rockefeller Foundation. Foundations contribute billions to colleges, universities, hospitals, libraries, museums, and research centers, but are poorly understood, even by the organizations receiving their grants.

Much of the information on foundations is elementary and anecdotal, found in directories, fund raising handbooks, and tales among grantseekers. Some manuals promise to reveal the "secrets" of foundations, much like paperbacks which offer miracle methods to lose weight, get rich, or break 80 in golf. Directories of foundations provide important data on assets, grants, programs, and priorities, but the information is necessarily abbreviated. Many grantseekers confess to knowing little about foundations, and what they do know, they learned mainly from handbooks. Still other grantseekers learned by trial and error, making such mistakes as writing proposals in jargon, sending the same proposal to multiple foundations simultaneously, or trying to manipulate foundation staff or trustees.

The contributions of foundations to American life, especially higher education, and the paradoxically poor understanding of foundations are the reasons I wrote this book. In so doing, I had three goals. My first purpose was to synthesize approximately 100 years of the literature on foundations, a body of works dating to 1875 and the founding of the Peabody Education Fund, the first modern American foundation. In fulfilling this purpose, I wanted to try to show what we know and, more importantly, do not know about foundations.

My second goal was to help grantseekers better understand foundations. I worked as a development officer for a social agency, two colleges, and a university, and I made all the mistakes grantseekers make with foundations. Later, as a management consultant, I saw other organizations make the same errors. From these experiences, I formed a view which influences this book. I believe that the training of grantseekers incorrectly emphasizes technical skill at the expense of substantive knowledge. Fund raising workshops almost always focus on such narrow topics as researching foundations and writing proposals, but rarely cover more meaningful subjects such as the principles that foundations apply in the grantmaking decision.

My third purpose was to let the people of foundations speak for themselves, for their words are powerful testimony requiring little interpretation, least of all by me. Although the book appropriately incorporates the findings of researchers on foundations, it relies on the first-person accounts of foundation trustees and staff. The words (and actions) of foundation people are the best evidence of their attitudes on such issues as accessibility, regulation, and relations with grantseekers. Their statements best disclose the difficulty of giving money away wisely and the isolation, subjectivity, and ambiguity of the process. Their testimony best illustrates how they apply subtle principles to try to correctly decide who shall and shall not receive a grant.

The book has seven chapters. Chapter one examines the twofold context of the study: the lack of information on foundations and the decline of foundation support of higher education. In 1935, one observer considered the lack of information on foundations to be their most significant characteristic. Fifty years later, another scholar reported that foundations remained "little known and less understood." From 1920, when foundation funding patterns were first recorded, to 1979, education, especially higher education, was the leading recipient of foundation funds, outpacing health, humanities, religion, science, social science, and welfare, the six other fields of funding interest monitored by The Foundation Center. In 1980, however, education fell to third place among the seven fields of interest where it stayed through the mid-1980s due partially to the changing priorities of foundations.

Chapter two explains the method of the study, defines qualitative research and data, and discusses the technique of synthesizing qualitative data. The criteria of representativeness, usefulness, and reliability are presented, as are the research processes of content analysis and coding. Publication and subjective variables in the literature on foundations are identified, and the convergence of themes is discussed. Chapter two concludes with a presentation of the characteristics of works in approximately 100 years of the literature on foundations.

Chapter three presents highlights of the historical relationship of foundations and higher education since the turn of the century and the founding of the General Education Board in 1902. The chapter also cites landmark contributions to higher education by other foundations including the Carnegie Corporation, the Ford Foundation, and the Carnegie Foundation for the Advancement of Teaching.

Chapter four reviews the quantitative, accessibility, and personnel dimensions of foundations. Narrative and tabular data are presented on the number, types, assets, grants, location, and funding patterns of foundations in the 1980s, borrowing heavily from the *Foundation Directory*. The accessibility dimension examines the record of communication by foundations with grantseekers, the federal government, and the general public. The inaccessibility of foundations and their unwillingness to communicate openly have been persistent criticisms since the 1950s when Congress began to find evidence of their secrecy. The personnel dimension discusses the personal, educational, and professional characteristics of foundation staff, as well as the number of women in foundations and the scarcity, recruitment, attitudes, and attributes of foundation staff.

Chapter five describes the difficulty of grantmaking, a complex process which is neither completely objective nor totally arbitrary. Grantmaking criteria are rarely discussed publicly by foundations, although evidence of the use of such benchmarks dates at least to the early 1900s. Many laymen believe that giving money away must be easy, but doing so wisely, according to an officer of the Ford Foundation, is "vexing to the soul and wearing on the liver" (Macdonald 1956). Grantmaking can be exhilarating, boring, fulfilling, or frustrating, all at the same time. People who do it well are rare, for the task requires a mixture of subjectivity and objectivity, empathy and detachment, intellect and instinct.

Chapter six examines the principles which foundations apply in making grants. Although grantmaking is their most important activity, it has received little attention in the literature, despite the fact that understanding how foundations make grants has important benefits for both grantseekers and grantmakers. The observations of foundation trustees and staff on grantmaking are presented, and a theory of foundation grantmaking is proposed based on six principles: investment, competence, realism, clarity, continuity, and trust.

Chapter seven is a summary of the findings of the study with recommendations for improving five areas: research on philanthropy, the grantseeking practices of organizations, the accessibility of foundations, the recruitment of foundation staff, and the partnership of foundations and higher education.

Hollidaysburg, Pennsylvania
January 1990

I

PURPOSE AND CONTEXT
OF THE STUDY

"The most amazing thing about foundations is that so few people—
even informed and intelligent people—know about them."

> Robert Lester
> "The Philanthropic Endowment in
> Modern Life"
> *South Atlantic Quarterly* (1935)

"(Foundations) remain little known and less understood, shrouded in
mystery, inspiring in some the highest hopes and expectations and in
others dark fears and resentments."

> Waldemar Nielsen
> *The Golden Donors* (1985)

Purpose of the Study

Foundations and Higher Education is a description of the characteristics, accessibility, personnel, and grantmaking philosophy of
foundations. The study is directed primarily to administrators of
colleges and universities, but may benefit other organizations seeking
foundation funds.

1

The study has two purposes. First, the study seeks to assemble basic information on foundations, for the lack of such information has been a problem for over 50 years. Lester (1935), Hollis (1938), Kiger (1954), Macdonald (1956), Cheit and Lobman (1979), Broce (1981), Nielsen (1985), Payton (1985), Plinio (1986), Read (Desruisseaux 1986e), and Fox (1987) are among the scholars who have noted the scarcity of information on foundations.

The second purpose of the study is to identify the principles which foundations apply in grantmaking. This purpose is difficult because foundations do not often publicly discuss the grantmaking process. Kennedy (1974), former Editor of *Foundation News*, reports that foundations "rarely articulate . . . the more philosophical principles or guidelines that (they apply) to grant making." Much of foundation grantmaking is "secret or at least not public," adds Friedman (1973), and the process by which foundations choose grantees is "rarely described" (Odendahl and Boris 1983b).

Despite limited public discussion of the grantmaking process, evidence suggests that foundations do apply principles in grantmaking. At the first meeting of the Rockefeller Foundation in 1913, a "Memorandum on Principles" was developed to establish grantmaking policies (Fosdick 1952). Among the six principles outlined by the trustees were:

> Individual charity and relief are not to be considered. Preventive projects are to be preferred over projects of a palliative type. (And) no permanent good (may) be anticipated by giving aid for any purpose that is incapable of provoking a desire on the part of the recipient to assist and carry it forward (Fosdick 1952).

At the meeting, according to Weaver (1967), one imaginative trustee is reported to have added, "Our policy should be to have no policy."

In 1979, Warm observed an "increasing commitment" in foundations to discussing the grantmaking process, noting that many grantseekers have "serious misconceptions" about foundation grantmaking. The Council on Foundations first recommended grantmaking principles in 1980, urging its members to make grant decisions "clear and logical" and establish "basic policies (which) define program interests." Four years later, the Council issued a second set of principles, explaining that such policies provide a framework for "consistent, effective" grantmaking and inform grantseekers of the "ethical and philosophical values" of foundations (1984a, 1984b). The Council (1984b) also reported that foundations had begun to develop "operating principles," an achievement which Viscusi (1985b) attributes to increased professionalism of trustees and staff.

Context of the Study

The study emerges from two developments in the relationship of foundations and higher education. First, foundation support of higher education is decreasing relative to the gifts of other private donors. The Council for Financial Aid to Education has measured voluntary support of higher education since 1949, and from 1949 to 1969, foundations led all private donors, providing nearly one-fourth of all voluntary aid. However, since 1970, the foundations' share of private aid has decreased, and foundations now rank fourth behind alumni, friends ("non-alumni individuals"), and corporations, outpacing only religious denominations and consortia. (This study combines the two donor groups called religious denominations and consortia because their gifts are limited.) In 1979, ten years after the beginning of the decrease in foundations' share of aid, foundations had dropped to third position behind alumni and friends, but ahead of corporations and the religious denominations and consortia groups. Five years later in 1984, foundations had dropped to fourth position, leading only the religious denominations and consortia.

The second development in the relationship of foundations and higher education is the general failure of higher education to respond to the decline of foundation support, a problem which may be related to higher education's lack of understanding of foundations. Academic leaders such as Bernstein, Bunting, Kerr, Marchese, and Newman have noted the failure of higher education to reply to the decrease in foundation aid, and Payton, former Director of the Exxon Education Foundation, contends that the higher education disciplines have "sort of gone off and isolated themselves" (Sleeper 1985). Foundation officials including Hamburg of the Carnegie Corporation, Furman of the MacArthur Foundation, Sawyer of the A. W. Mellon Foundation, and Stanley of the Ford Foundation have also noted higher education's weak response to the decrease in foundation aid (Sleeper 1985). Many officers in both higher education institutions and foundations attribute the poor response to higher education's inadequate understanding of foundations. Plinio (1986), President of the Prudential Foundation, indicates that "little is known and understood" about foundations, while Boris (1985), Vice President of Research for the Council on Foundations, believes that the need for research on foundations is "more compelling with every passing year." Read, Vice President of the Foundation Center, which publishes the *Foundation Directory*, adds that the "low level" of understanding of foundations is "one of the biggest constant challenges we face" (Desruisseaux 1986e). Higher education researchers including Cheit and Lobman (1979) and Broce (1981) have also observed the academy's poor response to the decrease of foundation aid and believe that the partnership of foundations and higher education has been weakened.

Foundations and Higher Education Income

Among the private donors to higher education, none has perhaps had greater influence than foundations. Cheit and Lobman (1979) report that foundations produced standards for courses and credits, developed faculty pensions, increased salaries for teaching and research, and pioneered educational opportunities for women and blacks. "In short," write Cheit and Lobman (1979), "foundation money and vision have had profound effect on the transformation of higher education into its modern form. . . ."

The contributions of foundations to higher education are remarkable in light of the relatively small sums involved. Even at the peak of their grants to higher education, between 1915 and 1920 when large awards were made for capital purposes, foundation grants represented "no more than 10 percent" of the income of colleges and universities (Cheit and Lobman 1979). Although foundations may once have provided a tenth of higher education income, they now contribute a much smaller share of current funds. As shown on Table 1, between 1950 and 1985, foundation grants averaged just 1.7 percent of the current fund income of colleges and universities and declined from a high of 2.8 percent in 1959–60 to 1.2 percent in 1984–85.

Foundations and Voluntary Support

Although contributing a minority of the current fund income of higher education, foundations have long been a major source of voluntary support. Between 1950 and 1986, as shown on Table 2, foundations provided nearly 22 percent of voluntary support to higher education. During the 1950s, foundations contributed nearly $1.2 billion, or 23.6 percent of voluntary support. In the 1960s, foundations gave over $3.0 billion, or 24.4 percent of voluntary aid. In the 1970s, foundations granted nearly $5.4 billion, or 22.7 percent of voluntary support. In the 1980s, foundations contributed nearly $7.5 billion, or 20.0 percent of voluntary support of higher education.

Table 1

Foundation Grants as a Percentage of the Current Fund Income of All Higher Education Institutions, 1949–50 to 1984–85

Year	Current Fund Income (Millions)	Foundation Grants Amount (Millions)	Foundation Grants Percent of Current Fund Income
1949–50	$ 2,375	$ 60	2.5
1959–60	5,786	163	2.8
1969–70	21,515	434	2.0
1979–80	58,520	903(a)	1.5
1980–81	65,585	922	1.4
1981–82	72,191	1,003	1.4
1982–83	79,452	1,018	1.3
1983–84	86,537	1,081	1.3
1984–85	$94,732	$1,175	1.2

(a): Includes a $105 million nonrecurring transfer for unrestricted endowment. In 1978–79, foundation grants were $701 million.

Source: American Council on Education, *Fact Book on Higher Education: 1984–85* (1984); Council for Financial Aid to Education, *Voluntary Support of Education: 1985–86* (1987); United States Department of Education, *Financial Statistics of Higher Education Institutions*, selected years

Table 2

Foundation Grants as a Percentage of Voluntary Support to All Higher Education Institutions, by Decade, 1949–50 to 1985–86

Decade	Total Voluntary Support (Millions)	Foundation Grants Amount (Millions)	Foundation Grants Percent of Total Voluntary Support
1950s	$ 4,906	$ 1,160	23.6
1960s	12,650	3,082	24.4
1970s	23,650	5,362	22.7
1980s(a)	37,370	7,465	20.0
1949–50 to 1985–86	$78,576	$17,069	21.7

(a): through 1985–86

Source: Council for Financial Aid to Education, *Voluntary Support of Education, 1985–86* (1987)

Despite representing nearly 22 percent of voluntary support from 1950 to 1986, foundation grants have declined relative to the gifts of other private donors. As shown on Table 3, foundations decreased their share of aid by 15 percent from the 1950s to the 1980s. Over

Table 3

Voluntary Support of Higher Education from Major Donor Groups, by Decade, 1949–50 to 1985–86 (Millions)

Decade	Alumni		Friends		Foundations	
	Dollars	Percent Share	Dollars	Percent Share	Dollars	Percent Share
1950s	$ 1,066	21.7	$ 1,156	23.6	1,160	23.6
1960s	2,833	22.4	3,050	24.1	3,082	24.4
1970s	5,576	23.6	5,818	24.6	5,362	22.7
1980s(a)	9,206	24.2	8,654	23.2	7,465	20.0
Total	$18,681	23.8	$18,678	23.8	$17,069	21.7
Percent Change: 1950 to 1986	11.5		(1.7)		(15.3)	

Decade	Corporations		Religious/Consortia	
	Dollars	Percent Share	Dollars	Percent Share
1950s	$ 644	13.1	$ 880	17.9
1960s	1,978	15.6	1,707	13.5
1970s	3,723	15.7	3,171	13.4
1980s(a)	8,109	21.7	4,118	11.0
Total	$14,454	18.4	$9,876	12.6
Percent Change: 1950 to 1986	65.7		(38.6)	

(a): through 1985–86

Source: Council for Financial Aid to Education, *Voluntary Support of Education, 1985–86* (1987)

Table 4

Rank of Sources of Voluntary Support to Higher Education, by Decade, 1949–50 to 1985–86

Rank in 1950s	Donor Group	Dollars (Millions)	Percent Share
1	Foundations	$1,160	23.6
2	Friends	1,156	23.6
3	Alumni	1,066	21.7
4	Religious/Consortia	880	17.9
5	Corporations	$ 644	13.1

Table 4 (continued)

Rank in 1980s	Donor Group	Dollars (Millions)	Percent Share
1	Alumni	$9,026	24.2
2	Friends	8,654	23.2
3	Corporations	8,109	21.7
4	Foundations	7,465	20.0
5	Religious/Consortia	$4,118	11.0

Source: Council for Financial Aid to Education, *Voluntary Support of Education, 1985–86* (1987)

the same period, however, alumni increased their share by over 11 percent and corporations increased their share by 66 percent. Religious denominations and consortia decreased their share by 39 percent, while the share of aid from friends fell 2 percent. However, the most important decrease was that of foundations, for their 15 percent decline in share represents the largest revenue loss. From 1950 to 1986, foundation grants totalled over $17 billion, nearly 73 percent more than the gifts of religious denominations and consortia, whose share also slipped noticeably. Moreover, the foundations' 22 percent share of aid over the four decades is nearly double the 13 percent share of religious denominations and consortia.

The decrease in the foundations' share of voluntary support has occurred primarily in the past ten years. As shown on Table 5, foundations had the second smallest percentage of increase in aid among the five donor groups between 1976 and 1986. Moreover, since 1976, the increase in foundation grants was 18 percent below the average increase of the five donor groups and 19 percent below the increase in total voluntary aid. From 1981 to 1986, foundations again had the second lowest percentage of increase in aid among the five donor groups. Also, since 1981, the increase in foundation grants was nearly 30 percent below the average increase of the five donor groups and 31 percent below the increase in total voluntary support.

The decrease in foundation support over the past ten years is more striking than depicted because of a single gift of $100 million in 1986 by the Danforth Foundation to Washington University. If the gift of $100 million is excluded, foundation grants in 1986 would drop from $1.36 billion to $1.26 billion. From 1976 to 1986, with the $100 million gift excluded, foundations would still rank fourth in the percentage of increase in voluntary aid among the five donor groups. However, from 1981 to 1986, with the $100 million gift excluded, foundations would rank last among the five donor groups in the percentage of increase in voluntary aid.

Table 5

Percent Increases in Voluntary Support of Higher Education from Major Donor Groups, 1976–77 to 1985–86 (Millions)

	Total Voluntary Support	Alumni	Friends	Foun- dations	Corpo- rations	Religious/ Consortia
1985–86	$7,400	$1,825	$1,781	$1,363	$1,702	$729
1976–77	$2,670	$ 638	$ 646	$ 558	$ 446	$382
Percent Increase: 1985–86 over 1976–77	177.2	186.1	175.7	144.3	281.6	90.8

	Rank	Donor Group	Percent Increase
Rank of Percent Increases: 1985–86 over 1976–77	1	Corporations	281.6
	2	Alumni	186.1
	3	Friends	175.7
	4	Foundations	144.3
	5	Religious/Consortia	90.8

	Total Voluntary Support	Alumni	Friends	Foun- dations	Corpo- rations	Religious/ Consortia
1985–86	$7,400	$1,825	$1,781	$1,363	$1,702	$729
1981–82	$4,860	$1,240	$1,097	$1,003	$ 976	$544
Percent Increase: 1985–86 over 1981–82	52.3	47.2	62.4	35.9	74.4	34.0

	Rank	Donor Group	Percent Increase
Rank of Percent Increases: 1985–86 over 1981–82	1	Corporations	74.4
	2	Friends	62.4
	3	Alumni	47.2
	4	Foundations	35.9
	5	Religious/Consortia	34.1

Source: Council for Financial Aid to Education, *Voluntary Support of Education, 1985–86* (1987)

Reasons for the Decline of Foundation Support

There are five main reasons for the decline of foundation support of higher education. First, when adjusted for inflation, foundation assets showed virtually no growth from 1962 to 1982. Rudney

(1987) examined foundation assets from 1962 to 1982 by studying a sample of 367 foundations, each of which had 1982 assets of at least $5 million. Although the assets of the 367 foundations increased 220 percent over the twenty years from $11.5 billion to $36.8 billion, the growth rate when adjusted for inflation was "virtually zero" (Rudney 1987). Odendahl (1987a) confirms that from the early 1970s to 1983, foundation assets declined as a share of the general economy, and their value when adjusted for inflation showed no growth. Between 1972 and 1975, foundation assets decreased sharply, followed by a slight decline from 1975 to 1981. From 1981 to 1985, foundation assets increased, mainly because of strong investment performance and less stringent federal regulations on the "pay-out" rate of grants (Odendahl 1987a). Tivnan (1984) cites the Ford Foundation, the world's largest, as an example of the decline of foundation assets. After a sluggish stock market in the 1970s reduced the assets of the Ford Foundation from $4.1 billion to $1.7 billion, President Franklin Thomas decreased staff and grants by more than half. Said Thomas: "No foundation can do as much as it used to" (Tivnan 1984). In the 1970s, explains Nielsen (1985), "shocking losses" were suffered by many foundations, and the "gigantic bath" resulted from both the stock market and "inept investment management." At the Ford Foundation, Nielsen (1985) confirms that assets experienced "well over a 50 percent loss," and that when Thomas became President, Ford had some "800 staff members worldwide." By 1985, Ford Foundation staff numbered approximately 500, and grantmaking and administrative costs had been "reduced accordingly" (Nielsen 1985).

Since the early 1980s, foundation assets have increased, but the sudden drop in the stock market on October 19, 1987 offset part of the gain (*The Chronicle of Higher Education,* November 18, 1987). The Rockefeller Foundation, for example, reported an 18 percent asset loss after the October 1987 stock market drop, while the Kellogg Foundation suffered a 20 percent loss (McMillen 1987b). The Ford Foundation averted losing significant assets on October 19, 1987 by reducing the proportion of stock in its portfolio from 60 to 40 percent earlier in the year. Ford's assets did fall 8 percent on October 19, but by two days later, the Foundation had recovered half its loss (McMillen 1987b). Although many foundations lost assets on October 19, 1987, some foundations do not consider the losses catastrophic. "We're not panicking," says Conner of the Lilly Endowment. "There have been other declines in our 50-year history, and these things tend to even out" (McMillen 1987b). However, recoveries and patience notwithstanding, foundation assets over the past two and half decades have shown little real growth, and their failure

Table 6

**Creation Rate of Independent Foundations with Assets of At Least
$1 Million, by Decade, Before 1910 to 1983**

Decade	Number Created	Percent Increase (Decrease) over Previous Decade	Total Population
Before 1910	51	—	—
1910 to 1919	44	(13.7)	95
1920 to 1929	108	145.5	203
1930 to 1939	164	51.9	367
1940 to 1949	571	248.2	938
1950 to 1959	1,120	96.2	2,058

Average Increase Over
Previous Decade: 1910 to 1959: 105.6

1960 to 1969	766	(31.6)	2,824
1970 to 1979	401	(47.7)	3,225
1980 to 1983	135	(66.3)	3,360

Average Decrease Over
Previous Decade: 1960 to 1983: (48.5)

Source: *America's Wealthy and the Future of Foundations* (1987)

to appreciate "belies the notion of an irreversible, ever expanding accumulation of wealth" (Nelson 1987).

The second reason for the decrease in foundation support of higher education is a reduction in the number of new foundations. During the first half of the twentieth century, the number of new foundations increased steadily, but the number of new foundations decreased in each of the last three decades. As shown on Table 6, the number of new foundations with at least $1 million in assets (an eligibility criterion for inclusion in the *Foundation Directory*) increased in every decade but one from before 1910 through 1959. Although the number of new, large foundations fell nearly 14 percent in the 1910s, the number increased over 145 percent in the 1920s. In the 1930s, the number of new, large foundations increased nearly 52 percent and rose almost 250 percent in the 1940s. In the 1950s, the number of new, large foundations nearly doubled over the 1940s. From before 1910 through 1959, 2,058 foundations with at least $1 million in assets were established, and the average decade increase in new foundations from 1910 through 1959 was over 105 percent.

From 1960 through 1983, the creation rate of large foundations

Table 7

Terminated Foundations of All Sizes, 1970 to 1982

Year	Number Terminated	Percent Increase (Decrease) over Previous Year
1970(a)	883	—
1971	1,506	70.6
1972	1,733	15.1
1973	946	(45.4)
1974	952	—
1975	792	(16.8)
1976	784	(1.0)
1977	618	(21.2)
1978	585	(32.2)
1979	616	5.3
1980	555	(14.9)
1981	455	(18.0)
1982	151	(66.8)
Total	10,576	

(a) The number of foundations which terminated before 1970 is not available from the Foundation Center.

Source: *America's Wealthy and the Future of Foundations (1987)*

decreased. In the 1960s, the formation rate fell nearly 32 percent from the 1950s, and in the 1970s, the number of new, large foundations decreased nearly 48 percent from the 1960s. From 1980 through 1983, the creation rate of large foundations fell over 66 percent from the 1970s. Although the formation rate of large foundations averaged over 105 percent per decade from 1910 through the 1950s, the rate averaged a negative 48.5 percent from 1960 to 1983.

The decline in the creation rate of large foundations since 1960 is compounded by the termination of over 10,000 foundations from 1970 through 1982. As shown on Table 7, 10,526 foundations of all sizes ceased operations between 1970 and 1982.

The third reason for the decline of foundation support is that foundations are redefining their general grantmaking mission, responding perhaps to Bolling's call as Chairman of the Council on Foundations for "A Time for Reassessment" (1978). Cheit and Lobman (1979) detected the reevaluation of mission by foundations, reporting that foundation officers are concerned with "identifying the foundation role (through) introspection and examination (in) all fields of grant making." The Institute for Educational Affairs, a conservative interest group formed by foundations in 1977, sponsored its first "Philanthropic Roundtable" in 1987 to enable foundations to "reflect more on what they are doing" and discuss grantmaking priorities with "greater scrutiny" (Desruisseaux 1987c). Lenkowsky, President of the Institute, explains that foundations are evaluating the "*effectiveness* of philanthropic support" as well as their objectives and accomplishments. Kennedy, President of the Joyce Foundation, explains that "when you have a philosophy behind your giving, you can make choices in a more definitive way," while Katz, President of the American Council of Learned Societies, believes that foundations have been "insufficiently critical (and) insufficiently reflective" of their priorities (Desruisseaux 1987c).

Marchese, Bernstein, and Newman (1985) contend that foundations are reevaluating interests because they now see themselves as "key agents in the nation's independent sector," a $200 billion collection of organizations that includes "everything from private hospitals and colleges to the Boy Scouts." As new partners in the independent sector, many foundations now have an "enlarged scope of vision as to what they should support" (Marchese, Bernstein, and Newman 1985). McMillen (1988) adds that government has assumed some of the traditional responsibilities of foundations, leaving them with "not quite the same sweeping impact." Ilchman, President of Sarah Lawrence College and a trustee of the Rockefeller Foundation, notes that foundations were once a more dominant source of charitable funds. "Now foundations are a bit player. The context has changed"(McMillen 1988).

The fourth reason for the decrease in aid is that foundations are changing their view of higher education. Observing a decrease in foundation grants to higher education in 1971, Cheit noted that "problems other than education . . . have attracted the interest of the large charitable foundations." Eight years later, Cheit and Lobman found a further reduction in foundation support of higher education, reporting that foundations are "not confident about their current role or its importance to the field." Kerr, perhaps higher education's foremost spokesman, agrees that foundations are decreasing their support of the academy. "(T)here's no question that higher education as an explicit focus of concern has faded somewhat for Ford, Rockefeller, Carnegie, and others. They're just less involved" (Sleeper 1985). Stanley of the Ford Foundation notes that foundations have a strong disposition to view education "incrementally," but not as an "ecology, a system in its own right" (Sleeper 1985). Bunting, President of Vassar College, adds that foundations have "reversed course" and now view higher education as a "means to other ends, rather than as an object for improvement within it-self" (Sleeper 1985). Dunham of the Carnegie Corporation confirms the impressions of Cheit, Lobman, Kerr, Stanley, and Bunting. "We've totally re-oriented our programs," reports Dunham. "There is no more higher education program. Our educational portfolio is science, technology, and the economy. . . ." (Sleeper 1985).

McMillen (1988) notes that the Rockefeller Foundation, after months of planning, now favors programs with "interconnected" themes. Previously, the Foundation heavily supported health and medicine. Today, however, the Foundation has "branched into other areas" including international development, science, agriculture, health, the arts and humanities, population studies, and equal opportunity. The Foundation no longer makes grants to higher education institutions, but rather, views colleges and universities as "tools to address the social problems it has identified" (McMillen 1988).

The fifth reason for the decline of foundation support of higher education is that corporations, whose gifts to the academy rose faster than those of any other private donor since 1976, are beginning to divert their funds to other forms of education, especially public elementary and secondary schools. A decade ago, reports Bailey (1988), the Atlantic Richfield Foundation gave "only to higher education." In 1987, however, the foundation gave over half its $11.5 million in grants to pre-college programs, awarding only one new grant to colleges—$709,000 to recruit and train black and Hispanic students in science, business, and engineering. Wilson, Director of the ARCO Foundation, explains that its support of minorities is "no longer social awareness. It's . . . survival and necessity" (Bailey 1988). A January 1988 survey showed that two-thirds of 130 major corporations listed primary and secondary education as their top priority. Two years earlier, 42 percent of the corporations had ranked primary and secondary education as their main interest. In both the 1986 and 1988 surveys, higher education ranked fourth in priority (Bailey 1988). The number of companies which match employee gifts to primary and secondary schools is further evidence of increasing corporate support for pre-college education. From 1982 to 1987, the number of corporations matching employee gifts to elementary and secondary schools increased 25 percent from 374 to 465 (Bailey 1988). The Amoco Foundation expected to award over 15 percent of its 1988 budget to pre-college programs, up from less than 1 percent five years ago, while the General Electric Foundation planned to award over 15 percent of its grants in 1988 to pre-college programs, up from 5 percent in 1982. Says Ostergard, President of the General Electric Foundation, "Any spare dollar I can put my hands on is going to pre-college programs." The Honeywell Foundation announced its first pre-college program in 1985, and Hoven, the Foundation's Director, adds, "We expect our pre-college support to go way up this year" (Bailey 1988). Willis, Director of the Bell-South Foundation, which has also begun to fund elementary and secondary schools, is critical of college schools of education, contending that if colleges "had been doing their job in the first place," primary and secondary schools would be in better condition. Shalala, Chancellor of the University of Wisconsin, is encouraging corporations to fund elementary and secondary schools, rather than trying to persuade them to fund higher education. Children in elementary and secondary schools, she argues, will "shape colleges' future far more than anyone now enrolled" (Bailey 1988). The Alcoa Foundation, which is also increasing its support of pre-college programs, planned to reduce its share of 1988 grants reserved for higher education from 50 to 40 percent. Gadbery, Director of the Alcoa Foundation, places the new emphasis on pre-college programs in perspective, reporting that the demands for corporate support have risen sharply in recent years. Says Gadbery: "There's no question that it is becoming more competitive for colleges" (Bailey 1987).

The decline of foundation support is related not only to decreasing assets and new priorities of foundations, but also to three recent developments in higher education finance. The first development is that since the 1950s, public sources of income have replaced private sources as the predominant supplier of higher education revenue. Second, since the late 1960s, discretionary revenue, the venture capital of higher education, has steadily declined as a share of the income of colleges and universities. Third, since the late 1960s, a "new depression" (Cheit 1971, 1973) has occurred in higher education because income has failed to keep pace with costs.

Shifting Sources of Income: The First Development

As shown on Table 8, between 1930 and 1940, private sources of revenue including tuition and fees, endowment income, and philanthropic support comprised nearly 60 percent of higher education income. However, since 1960, public sources have provided no less than 60 percent of the income of colleges and universities. Commenting on financial developments in the academy, the Carnegie Council on Policy Studies concludes that the "most noticeable feature is the rise in the relative importance of public versus private financing of colleges and universities since World War II" (1980).

Table 8

Sources of Income to All Higher Education Institutions for Educational and General Purposes, 1929–30 to 1980–81

Year	Total Income (Millions)	Percent from Public Sources	Percent from Private Sources
1929–30	$ 410	41.8	58.2
1939–40	527	40.7	59.3
1949–50	— Data Not Reported —		
1959–60	4,337	59.6	40.4
1969–70	16,200	63.9	36.1
1976–77	32,281	63.1	36.9
1980–81	$49,959	63.3	36.7

Source: Carnegie Council on Policy Studies in Higher Education, *Three Thousand Futures* (1980) and American Council on Education, *Fact Book on Higher Education: 1984–85* (1984)

The Loss of Venture Capital: The Second Development

The second recent financial development in higher education is the decline of discretionary revenue. Kramer (1980) defines discretionary revenue as the endowment income and private gifts and grants received by higher education institutions. He considers discretionary revenue to be the venture capital of higher education, the margin of financing that promotes the "creative health" of colleges and universities, making possible "robust health over and above sheer survival." Creative health, writes Kramer (1980), is the ability of higher education institutions to "adapt, take risks, and give operational expression to autonomously developed ideas about what they should strive to accomplish." Without sufficient discretionary revenue, colleges and universities "run the risk of becoming publicly owned utilities" (Kramer 1980). As shown on Table 9, from 1930 to 1985, discretionary revenue declined by nearly 57 percent as part of the current fund income of colleges and universities.

The "New Depression": The Third Development

The third major financial development in higher education is the "new depression" (Cheit 1971, 1973) in which institutional income has failed to keep pace with costs. Cheit (1971) studied the financial condition of 41 representative colleges and universities, finding that 29 institutions (71 percent) were "headed for financial trouble or were in financial difficulty." The main reason for the problem, ac-

Table 9

Discretionary Revenue of All Higher Education Institutions as a Percentage of Current Fund Income, 1930 to 1985

Year	Current Fund Income (Millions)	Discretionary Revenue (Millions)	Percent Discretionary of Current Fund Income
1929–30	$ 555	$ 95	17.1
1939–40	715	112	15.7
1949–50	2,375	215	9.1
1959–60	5,786	590	10.2
1969–70	21,515	1,449	6.7
1979–80	58,520	3,985	6.8
1980–81	65,585	4,541	6.9
1981–82	72,191	5,160	7.2
1982–83	79,452	5,773	7.3
1983–84	86,537	6,289	7.3
1984–85	$94,732	$6,993	7.4

Percent Change: 1930 to 1985: (56.7)
Percent Change: 1960 to 1985: (27.5)

Source: American Council on Education, *Fact Book on Higher Education: 1984–85* (1984) and United States Department of Education, *Financial Statistics of Higher Education Institutions*, selected years

cording to Cheit (1971), is a "declining rate of income growth, and in some cases an absolute decline in income" which began in the latter 1960s. Cheit explains that

> costs and income are both rising (but) costs are rising at a steady or slowly growing rate . . . whereas income is growing at a declining rate (due to) declining growth rates in federal government support, gifts and grants, and endowment income (1971).

Cheit (1971) learned that one-quarter of all private colleges were using endowment to meet operating expenses, while Jellema (1971) found that 20 percent of private colleges with less than 500 students were running annual operating deficits. Sixteen percent of private institutions with 500 to 1,000 students had yearly operating deficits (Jellema 1971).

Two years after his 1971 study, Cheit revisited his sample of 41 colleges and universities, finding that the institutions had reached a "plateau of fragile stability." Cheit explains that if neither "exhortation, rebellion, or a new outside world" can make colleges or universities change, it is clear that a "shortage of money can" (1973). However, despite the progress made by the 41 colleges and universities, Cheit warned that the

Table 10

**Percentage of Institutions Experiencing a Revenue Shortfall from
1980 to 1984, by Control of Institution**

Control of Institution	Percent with Revenue Shortfall
All Institutions	45
Public Institutions	49
Private Institutions	42

Source: American Council on Education, *Conditions Affecting College and University Financial Strength* (1985)

basis for rejoicing over the more stabilized current situation is quite limited. It is, for some institutions, a situation of genuine stability, but there is a continued downward movement for an equal number, and in some cases, there is serious financial trouble ahead (1973).

In 1985, Anderson examined the financial condition of 438 higher education institutions in response to the U.S. Education Department's concern that a "large number of colleges may be in financial stress." As shown on Table 10, 45 percent of the surveyed institutions said that they had suffered a "revenue shortfall" between 1980 and 1984.

Respondents which experienced a revenue shortfall were asked to rate thirty-eight management strategies on their value in improving financial conditions. Ratings ranged from five ("highly beneficial impact") to one ("low beneficial impact"). Only ten of the thirty-eight strategies were used by a third or more of the institutions, and only five of the ten were given high scores (four or five) by a majority of the respondents. Table 11 shows that the highest-rated strategy was "increased fund raising efforts," as 69 percent of the institutions with a revenue shortfall used this strategy and 62 percent gave it a usefulness rating of four or five.

Anderson (1985) also found that half or more of the 438 institutions surveyed used four "management practices" to offset the revenue shortfall; 1) long-range planning; 2) program review; 3) cash management; and 4) a central contingency fund. As shown on Table 12, cash management was the practice most often used by the surveyed institutions, and its usefulness score of 4.1 was the highest awarded.

Keller (1983), who also studied the financial condition of colleges and universities, reports that a "specter . . . of decline and bankruptcy" is haunting higher education, and that by 1995, "10 to 30 percent" of America's colleges may "close their doors or merge with other institutions." In short, concludes Keller (1983), finance domi-

Table 11

Highly-Rated Management Strategies in Offsetting Revenue Shortfalls, 1980 to 1984

Management Strategy	Percentage of Shortfall Institutions Using the Strategy	Percentage of High Ratings (4 or 5)
1) Increased fund raising efforts	69	62
2) Increased student retention	67	49
3) Increased student recruitment	67	62
4) Increased student aid	49	52
5) Decreased faculty size	45	53
6) Increased class size	38	61
7) Decreased academic support staff	38	36
8) Decreased administrative staff	36	24
9) Decreased maintanance staff	35	22
10) Increased adult and evening classes	34	47

Source: American Council on Education, *Conditions Affecting College and University Financial Strength* (1985)

nates campus management, and higher education is "driven by financial concerns of the near future."

Higher Education's Response to Declining Foundation Support

The decrease in foundation aid to the academy has received little attention in the literature, and higher education has generally failed to make a constructive response to the decline. Marchese, Bernstein, and Newman (1985) believe that higher education's poor reply may be attributable to the "new names" in colleges and foundations, for

Table 12

Percentage of Use and Usefulness Ratings of Four Management Practices in Offsetting Revenue Shortfalls, 1980 to 1984

Management Practice	Percentage Using Practice	Percentage Rating Usefulness	Average Score (1 to 5)
1) Cash Management	73	70	4.1
2) Program Review	70	64	3.9
3) Long-Range Planning	75	60	3.8
4) Contingency Fund	51	48	3.8

Source: American Council on Education, *Conditions Affecting College and University Financial Strength* (1985)

many of their officers, who jointly developed projects in the 1960s and 1970s, have "retired or moved on to other pursuits." Stanley of the Ford Foundation believes that the poor response is part of a larger problem in academe: "We depend on faculty and administrators to tell us what they'll need two or three years from now (but) one of the stunning things you encounter is the difficulty academics have thinking systematically. . . ." (Sleeper 1985). Broce (1981), former President of Phillips University and the Kerr Foundation, believes that higher education's poor understanding of foundations contributes to the problem. "Most laymen (in colleges), including most fund raisers, actually know very little about foundations." Johnson, Research Director of the Exxon Education Foundation, agrees: "We know more about higher education than higher education knows about us" (1985). Concludes Broce (1981):

> For too long, most grantseekers have identified foundations with frustration. A mystery has clouded the relationship between foundations and those who wished they knew how to get money from them. (This shortcoming) can be attributed to the resistance, partly the result of ignorance, to communicate openly.

Higher education's poor response to the decline of foundation support may also be attributable to the general inaccessibility of foundations. Dickinson (1973), a university grantseeker, explains that

> too many foundations do not communicate with consumers, their own communities . . . or with anyone else. . . . Many have never published reports (and) many do not even acknowledge receipt of correspondence. . . .

Rockefeller (1973) explains that foundations often consider themselves "strictly private institutions immune from public . . . accountability," and Nielsen (1985) believes that foundations are "institutions like no others," operating in a "unique degree of abstraction from external pressures and controls," according to their own "largely self-imposed rules."

Lack of information on foundations has been a problem for over fifty years. Lester (1935) writes that the most striking feature of foundations is that so few people understand them. In 1938, Hollis attempted a literature search on foundations, but was unable to find a "single book on any phase of the work of philanthropic foundations." In 1952, a House Select Committee sent letters seeking information on foundations to 100 leaders in education, business, labor, and government. One third of the sample did not reply and two-fifths of the respondents made comments that were "so vague as to be of no value," saying that they "knew little about foundations" (*Letters from Various Individuals* 1952).

Andrews, in the preface to Kiger (1954), notes that there is "little ordered knowledge" on foundations, and although histories of individual foundations have appeared, "few attempts at a broader view have been made. Sources are regrettably fragmentary," he writes. "Broad, scholarly studies are lacking, and are needed." Kiger (1954) indicates that "no attempt . . . has been made to provide a systematic, historical interpretation of 20th century foundation thought. . . ." Macdonald (1956) also notes the lack of research on foundations, reporting that "surprisingly little" has been written about foundations, and much of the literature is "very specialized and technical or else superficial and sensationalized."

If grantseekers lack an understanding of foundations, Congressional hearings for the Tax Reform Act of 1969 showed that the foundation community was "ignorant of the facts about itself" (Nielsen 1985). Nielsen believes that in the late 1960s and early 1970s, foundations were "intellectually moribund."

> There was little communication among foundations on philanthropic issues. There did not exist a recognized forum or publication for the candid discussion of problems (and) there was only the most rudimentary base of research data. . . . (1985).

Cheit and Lobman (1979) add that because "so little is known" about foundations, there has been "little empirical basis for judgment."

> Current information about foundations is so weak that a whole 'grantmanship' industry has sprung up to serve potential grantees. . . . The best information is largely based on grant descriptions in foundation annual reports . . . or on generalized, anecdotal, sometimes contradictory observations.

Boris (1985) believes that the need for research on foundations is "compelling," explaining that research has been hindered by the "absence of a focal point, of research stipends, and of forums for presenting and learning about related projects. . . ." Plinio (1986) agrees: "Now is the time for all of us (in) the nonprofit sector to become more involved in promoting the value of basic research . . . both on philanthropy and our sector." Adds Plinio:

> Without a focus on research, the sector is considered less important in the eyes of professional researchers, resulting in an absence of academic pursuit of our field. . . . We would like to introduce courses about philanthropy (but) currently there are no wholesale or fully supported attempts at developing and implementing this idea in a coherent manner (1986).

Read, Vice President of the Foundation Center, indicates that the "generally low level of knowledge and understanding of private foundations . . . is one of the biggest constant challenges we face" (Desruisseaux 1986e). Gadbery, Director of the Alcoa Foundation, notes that his work is "little understood" by college presidents and development officers seeking grants, and Bailey reports that "few grant seekers truly understand how a corporate-contributions program operates" (1987). Adds Payton (1985): "I have long been arguing for increased academic attention to the philanthropic tradition (but) few among the very best scholars have shown much interest in (these) knotty and untidy problems. . . ." Explains Payton:

> Philanthropy—in the limited sense of fund raising and grant making—is, after all, the means we use to call our priorities to wider attention, and to marshal the means to effect change. . . . The study of philanthropy also helps in the education of professionals who presume to serve others: those of us who make grants, and those of you who use them. . . . (1985).

Although several research centers on philanthropy have recently been established, Fox believes that foundations continue to be "under-studied and under-analyzed" (1987). Payton, therefore, is "convinced" that the study of foundations "calls for more serious academic attention" (1985).

Purpose Summary: Synthesis of Information on Foundations

The decline of foundation aid to higher education and the lack of research on foundations indicate the need for a synthesis of the literature on foundations for higher education administrators. From 1970 to 1986, the foundations' share of voluntary support decreased by 15 percent, with the majority of the decline occurring since 1976. In 1979, foundations, which had ranked first among the five private donor groups from 1949 to 1969, dropped to third position behind alumni and friends. In 1984, foundations fell to fourth position behind alumni, friends, and corporations, outpacing only the religious denominations and consortia. In 1986, foundations continued to rank fourth among the five donor groups.

A half-century of scholars, foundation executives, and higher education officers have noted the lack of information on foundations, citing the problem as an impediment to strengthening the partnership of foundations and the academy. A synthesis of the literature on foundations for higher education administrators is therefore timely, for such a study may improve the academy's understanding of foundations and facilitate a response to the decline of foundation support.

The Order of the Study

The study contains six additional chapters. Chapter Two defines the research method, explains the techniques of synthesis and integration, and discusses characteristics of the literature on foundations. Chapter Three describes the historical relationship of foundations and higher education, citing landmark foundation programs and the contributions of foundations to the development of higher education. Chapter Four describes the quantitative, personnel, and accessibility dimensions of foundations. Chapter Five examines the grantmaking process, focusing on its difficulty and providing evidence that foundations apply principles in grantmaking. Chapter Six identifies six principles which foundations apply in grantmaking, explaining the significance of each principle, while citing evidence of the development and rationale of the principles. Information in Chapters Five and Six on the difficulty and principles of foundation grantmaking is presented in the words of founders, trustees, and staff members of foundations dating to the 19th century. Chapter Seven, the final chapter, presents a summary of the findings of the study with recommendations for officers of foundations and higher education institutions.

II

METHOD OF THE STUDY AND REVIEW OF THE LITERATURE

"Where is the knowledge we have lost in information?"

T. S. Eliot
"The Rock"

Purpose of the Chapter

This chapter defines the method of the study, explains the principles of synthesizing qualitative data, and cites the characteristics of the literature on foundations. The chapter performs six main functions:

1) defines the nature of qualitative data according to *Qualitative Evaluation Methods* (Patton 1980), specifying the type and quantity of qualitative data in the study;
2) defines the importance of context in a review of qualitative data and cites three ways in which the context of the study is established;
3) discusses the importance of synthesis as a research method, citing its applicability to higher education practitioners;

4) identifies the two major steps in a synthesis of qualitative data as sampling and content analysis, citing the criteria used to select the literature and the variables used to code, compare, and analyze its content;

5) defines the techniques used to establish convergence among themes disclosed by content analysis of the literature; and

6) reviews the number, age, types, and themes of works in the literature on foundations.

METHOD OF THE STUDY

"A good integration ... shows how much is known in an area (and) how little is known. It sums up, but does not end. In this sense, it is only a beginning."

Kenneth Feldman
"Using the Work of Others"
Sociology of Education (1971)

Qualitative Research and Data

The study employs the qualitative method of research which strives to identify categories, dimensions, and general principles to understand the unifying nature of particular settings (Patton 1980). Qualitative data are *"detailed descriptions"* of situations, events, and people and *"direct quotations"* on their experiences, attitudes, and beliefs (Patton 1980). Qualitative data are best revealed in statements which disclose how people have organized their experiences and perceptions (Patton 1980).

The study examines the quantitative, accessibility, and personnel dimensions of foundations, as well as the process of grantmaking. The quantitative dimension was chosen to provide a basic description of foundations including their number, types, assets, grants, funding patterns, and periods of establishment. The accessibility dimension was selected to examine the interaction of foundations with grantseekers, the federal government, and the general public. The record of foundations publishing annual reports and disclosing information in the *Foundation Directory* is identified in the accessibility section, as are the attitudes of foundation trustees, staff, and grantees on accessibility. The personnel dimension was chosen to provide a description of the personal, educational, and professional characteristics of foundation staff, citing their number and distribution and the attributes required of foundation officers. Grantmaking, which was selected because it is the central function of foundations, is examined in two ways. First, the difficulty of wisely distributing charitable dollars is cited by philosophers, philanthropists, and foundation officers. Second, the grantmaking decision is identified as purposeful, thereby suggesting that foundations apply principles in their grant decisions. The study observes Patton's 1980 recommendation on using direct quotations by citing the observations of not only the founders, trustees, and staff members of foundations, but also journalists, university researchers, independent scholars, government officials, grantees, and individuals in philanthropic associations.

Establishing the Context of the Study

One of the fundamental principles of qualitative research is that the whole is greater than the sum of its parts. Therefore, an understanding of a problem's context is essential for understanding the problem (Patton 1980). For a research topic to be productive, there must be a "body of knowledge within which the problem may be placed" (Getzels 1968).

The context of the study is established in three ways. First, the study cites the decline of foundation support of higher education relative to the gifts of other private donors. Second, the study describes higher education's poor response to the decline, disclosing evidence of a lack of understanding of foundations by higher education officials. Third, the study relates the decrease in foundation aid to three financial developments in higher education:

1) the shift from private to public funding;
2) the "new depression" (Cheit 1971, 1973); and
3) the decline of discretionary revenue.

Synthesis of Qualitative Data

The study combines the qualitative research methods of Patton (1980) with a form of inquiry called synthesis. Feldman (1971) defines synthesis as the "large-scale review and integration of existing theory and research." Reiss (1969) explains that synthesis is important because scholars may do a disservice by failing to focus their research with the objective of "deliberately cumulating knowledge in (one) area." Feldman (1971) contends that synthesis is especially meaningful to practitioners because the method assembles information, thereby facilitating its access and application.

Despite the importance of synthesis, a well-developed literature on the technique does not exist. Jackson (1980) found that 39 books on research methods revealed "very little" explanation of the technique, and "none of the discussions exceeded two pages in length." Glass (1976) believes that methods are needed for the summarization of information, while Feldman (1971) indicates that there is "little formal or systematic analysis of either the methodology or the importance of this type of research." Jackson (1980) cites four reasons and consequences of the lack of methods for such research.

> First, the lack of methods appears to be largely the result of social scientists failing to give much thought to such methods. . . . Second, (the lack of methods) makes it difficult to have standards for judging the quality of integrative reviews. Third, it makes it difficult for graduate students to do competent research reviews. Fourth, the lack of research methods hinders the accumulation of valid knowledge from previous research.

Despite the short literature on synthesis, Glass (1976) indicates that before information can "persuade skeptics, influence policy (or) affect practice," it must be known and communicated. "Someone must organize it, integrate it (and) extract the message."

Sampling Qualitative Data

The first step in an integration of qualitative data is choosing the information to be synthesized. According to Feldman (1971), synthesis requires a "selection—or in the broadest sense of the term, a 'sampling' " of the literature. Because the written work of others constitutes the raw data for the integrator, the researcher begins with bibliographies, reviews, and other integrations (Feldman 1971). Although such collection procedures lead to many works, the process does not guarantee total coverage. Thus, researchers must sample as wide a range of information as possible to be reasonably comprehensive, for the "larger the sample . . . the more representative and trustworthy it is" (Feldman 1971).

Light and Pillemer (1984) identify four sampling strategies for reviews of qualitative data. First, researchers may attempt to include every available study, notwithstanding the impossibility of same. Second, researchers may stratify the sample by study characteristics, selecting studies of a certain type or period. Third, researchers may include only published studies, thereby eliminating many conference papers and fugitive works. Fourth, researchers may choose studies by acknowledged experts to capitalize on their accumulated wisdom. The study applied three criteria to select the works to be synthesized. First, if the sample is to be representative, it must be "as large as possible" (Jackson 1980). Second, if the sample is to be pertinent, it must contain information useful to practitioners. Third, if the sample is to be reliable, it must be comprised primarily of works by "acknowledged experts" (Light and Pillemer (1984).

The Criterion of Representativeness

The criterion of representativeness is fulfilled by synthesizing over 2,500 works on foundations from the following nine sources:

1) over 300 works in the bibliographies of thirty landmark studies on foundations (Table 13). The landmark studies are classics in the literature on foundations and represent a century of works on foundations;

2) nearly 1,500 articles in *Foundation News* magazine from 1970 through 1986 (fifteen articles per issue and six issues per year);

3) twenty works on the historical relationship of foundations and higher education;

4) 100 works in the grantseeking literature including thirty-six issues of *Currents,* the journal of the Council for the Advancement and Support of Education, from 1975 through 1986 and two issues of *Change* magazine devoted to foundations; namely, "On Foundations" (1978) and "Foundations: Are They Shortchanging Higher Education?" (1985);

5) ten editions of the *Foundation Directory* (1975 to 1985);

6) ten editions of *Voluntary Support of Education* of the Council for Financial Aid to Education (1976–1986);

7) three policy statements of the Council on Foundations: *Some General Principles and Guidelines for Grantmaking Foundations* (1973); *Recommended Principles and Practices for Effective Grantmaking* (1980); and *Principles and Practices for Effective Grantmaking* (1984);

8) surveys of the characteristics of foundation staff (Boris, et al 1980–1986); and

9) surveys by the Council on Foundations on the number of foundations publishing annual reports.

The Criterion of Usefulness

The criterion of usefulness is fulfilled in three ways. First, to provide basic information on foundations, the study cites their quantitative, accessiblity, and personnel dimensions. Second, the study

Table 13

Thirty Landmark Works on Foundations: 1875 to 1985		
Title	Author	Year
1. *Proceedings of the Trustees of the Peabody Education Fund*	—	1875
2. *The Gospel of Wealth and Other Essays*	Carnegie	1900
3. *"A Science of Giving" Annual Report of the Carnegie Corporation*	Pritchett	1922
4. *The Foundation: Its Place in American Life*	Keppel	1930
5. *Wealth and Culture*	Lindeman	1936
6. *Operating Principles of the Larger Foundations*	Kiger	1954
7. *Philanthropic Foundations*	Andrews	1956
8. *The Ford Foundation: The Men and the Millions*	Macdonald	1956
9. *The Story of the Rockefeller Foundation*	Fosdick	1952
10. *Foundations: Twenty Viewpoints*	Andrews, ed.	1965
11. *U.S. Philanthropic Foundations*	Weaver	1967
12. *Foundations: Their Power and Influence*	Wormser	1968
13. *Trusteeship and the Management of Foundations*	Young and Moore	1969
14. *Hearings before the Committee on Ways and Means on the Subject of Tax Reform*	U.S. Congress, House	1969
15. *Foundations Under Fire*	Reeves	1970
16. *Private Giving and Public Policy*	Peterson Commission	1970
17. *The Money Givers*	Goulden	1971
18. *Private Money and Public Service*	Cunninggim	1972
19. *The Big Foundations*	Nielsen	1972
20. *The Management of American Foundations*	Zurcher	1972
21. *The Foundation Administrator*	Zurcher and Dustan	1972
22. *The Future of Foundations*	Heimann, ed.	1973
23. *The Philanthropoids*	Whitaker	1974
24. *Giving in America*	Filer Commission	1975
25. *Trustees and the Future of Foundations*	Nason	1977
26. *The Handbook on Private Foundations*	Freeman	1981
27. *America's Voluntary Spirit*	O'Connell, ed.	1983
28. *Philanthropy in an Age of Transition*	Pifer	1984
29. *The Golden Donors*	Nielsen	1985
30. *Working in Foundations*	Odendahl, Boris, and Daniels	1985

examines the process of grantmaking, which is the main function of foundations and a key interest of grantseekers. Third, the study identifies six principles which foundations apply in their grantmaking decisions, criteria which may be useful to grantseekers in understanding foundations and acquiring foundation grants.

The Criterion of Reliability

The criterion of reliability is fulfilled by relying on the works of scholars and foundation officers to benefit from the "accumulated wisdom (of) acknowledged experts" (Light and Pillemer 1984). The study also relies on the research of individuals in foundation associations and philanthropic study commissions shown in Table 14.

Content Analysis and Coding

The second step in a review of qualitative data is content analysis, a method of "analyzing communications in a systematic . . . manner to measure variables" (Kerlinger 1973). Instead of observing people's behavior, interviewing them, or asking them to answer questionnaires, content analysis "asks questions of the communications" that people have produced (Kerlinger 1973). Thus, Kerlinger (1973) notes that the method is similar to interviews, scales, and other methods of observation, but instead of sampling a single group, content analysis examines "many samples of information from multiple sources."

As content analysis begins, notes Patton (1980), the investigator is "open to whatever emerges from the data." As the research progresses, however, patterns and major dimensions of interest emerge. Patton (1980) explains that

> *analysis* is the process of bringing order to the data, organizing what there is into patterns, categories, basic descriptive units. *Interpretation* involves attaching meaning . . . to the analysis (by) explaining descriptive patterns, and looking for relationships and linkages among descriptive dimensions.

Uncovering patterns, themes, and categories, writes Patton (1980), is a creative process requiring "considered judgements" about what is meaningful in the data. Because qualitative analysts do not have statistical tests to indicate when a pattern is significant, they must rely on their own "intelligence, experience, and judgement" (Patton 1980).

Coding is the process of establishing "typologies" to describe patterns that appear in the data (Patton 1980). The evaluator begins by

Table 14

| Foundation Associations, Study Commissions, and Related Organizations ||
Entity	Purposes and Major Contributions
1. Council on Foundations	a) represents foundations to the federal government and the public b) publishes policy statements on grantmaking c) conducts conferences to discuss issues affecting foundations
2. Foundation Center	a) represents foundations to grant-seekers b) publishes the *Foundation Directory* and other sourcebooks c) maintains regional libraries of information on foundations d) operates a computerized foundation search service
3. National Committee for Responsive Philanthropy	a) represents grantseekers to foundations b) encourages greater accessibility by foundations c) testifies before Congress on philanthropic issues
4. Commission on Foundations and Private Philanthropy	a) published *Private Giving and Public Policy* (1970), one of the first major studies on the impact of foundations
5. Commission on Private Philanthropy and Public Needs	a) published *Giving in America* (1975)
6. Council for Financial Aid to Education	a) compiles annual data on private gifts and grants to higher education and private secondary schools b) publishes the *Survey of Voluntary Support*
7. Council for the Advancement and Support of Education	a) represents fund raising, public relations, alumni relations, and grant officers in higher education institutions and secondary schools b) co-publisher of the *Survey of Voluntary Support* c) publishes *Currents,* a monthly journal for advancement professionals

looking for "recurring regularities" that can be sorted into categories. Explains Feldman (1971):

> The amount of information available in the typically tens or hundreds of research reports . . . would be overwhelming unless the integrator develops a systematic scheme for indexing, coding and retrieving this information.

Patton (1980) adds that data must be categorized, for "without classification there is chaos." Thus, simplifying the "complexity of reality" into a manageable classification model is the first objective of coding (Patton 1980). The second goal of coding, according to Feldman (1971), is to achieve comparability among studies by devising ways to meaningfully compare them. For example, Feldman and Newcomb's 1969 integration of studies on the impact of college on students used such comparability factors as "interests," "intellectual ability," "personality dimensions," and "politico-economic orientation." Glass, McGaw, and Smith (1981) identified publication date, publication form, and professional affiliation of the author as other coding categories. Berelson (1954) adds that "words" and "themes" are two important coding categories. The word is the smallest unit of comparability and is used by itemizing key words in studies. The theme is a useful, though more difficult unit which is often a sentence or proposition. Themes are useful because they are "ordinarily realistic and close to the original content" (Berelson 1954).

For each work in the study, data on twenty-six variables were recorded to establish comparability and categorize themes. As shown on Table 15, five of the variables are descriptive information on the studies themselves including author's profession, publication form, and publication date. These variables are called publication variables.

The remaining twenty-one variables are keywords which correspond to words or themes that appear regularly in the literature. The keyword references are called substantive variables and were chosen by the weight of their appearance in the studies. Table 16 defines the substantive variables and cites the number of pages in works synthesized on which material corresponding to the substantive variables appeared. For example, information on the accessibility of foundations appeared on 205 separate pages in works synthesized for the study.

The publication and substantive variables were coded and itemized using the data base program on Appleworks software and an Apple IIc computer expanded to 512K. The record layout for the variables had nine parts as shown in this example:

Table 15

Publication Variables of Comparability		
Publication Variables	Coding Category	Detail
1. Author	1-Last name 2-First name 3-Middle initial	
2. Author's Profession (at publication of study)	1-Scholar	a-University b-Independent
	2-Foundation Association	a-Researcher b-Administrator
	3-Foundation Founder 4-Foundation Trustee	
	5-Foundation Staff	a-Director b-Staff
	6-Donee Group Member 7-Journalist	
	8-Government	a-Official b-Committee
3. Publication Form	1-Book 2-Chapter in a book 3-Article in a journal 4-Monograph 5-Pamphlet 6-Conference paper 7-Dissertation or thesis 8-Interview	
4. Type of Work	1-Survey research	a-Questionnaire or personal interview
	2-Experiential Commentary	a-Observation by a founder, trustee, or staff member
	3-Analysis	a-Research by an author who is not a member of a foundation or a donee group
	4-Statistical/Reference	a-Quantitative data or directories
5. Publication Data	1–Month, date, year	

Table 16

Substantive Variables of Comparability

Substantive Variable	Description and Number of Pages in Works Synthesized Containing Information on Each Substantive Variable
1. Accessibility	a-Relating to the interaction of foundations with grantseekers, the federal government, and the public; disclosure in the *Foundation Directory;* secrecy of foundations (205 pages)
2. Causes of Decline	a-Relating to the causes of the decline of foundation support of higher education (58 pages)
3. Competence	a-Relating to the judgement foundations make on the ability of grantseekers (76 pages)
4. Continuity	a-Relating to the importance of the continuity of grant projects after grants end (69 pages)
5. Competition	a-Relating to the number of requests which foundations receive and the competition for funds among grantseekers (19 pages)
6. Difficulty	a-Relating to the difficulty of grantmaking; of wisely distributing charitable funds; of deciding between applicants (166 pages)
7. Foundations and Higher Education	a-Relating to the historical relationship of foundations and higher education (305 pages)
8. Founders	a-Relating to the characteristics, beliefs, and experiences of the founders of foundations (72 pages)
9. Grantmaking	a-Relating to the philosophies which influence grantmaking; contentions on the nature of the task of making grants (165 pages)
10. History	a-Relating to the history of individual foundations or foundations collectively (141 pages)
11. Integration	a-Relating to the method of conducting a review of qualitative data (37 pages)
12. Investment	a-Relating to the carefulness and purposefulness of foundation grantmaking (302 pages)
13. Lack of Research	a-Relating to the scarcity of information on foundations (58 pages)

Table 16 (continued)

Substantive Variable	Description and Number of Pages in Works Synthesized Containing Information on Each Substantive Variable
14. New Depression	a-Relating to the inability of higher education income to keep pace with expenditures (76 pages)
15. Quantitative	a-Relating to the number, types, assets, grants, and funding patterns of foundations (191 pages)
16. Realism	a-Relating to the practicality and reasonableness of applications and applicants (79 pages)
17. Sampling	a-Relating to the methods and practices of selecting data to be studied in an integrative review (31 pages)
18. Staff	a-Relating to the beliefs and characteristics of the staff members of foundations (292 pages)
19. Trustees	a-Relating to the beliefs and characteristics of the trustees of foundations (163 pages)
20. Venture Capital	a-Relating to the decline of discretionary revenue in higher education (43 pages)
21. Voluntary Support	a-Relating to gifts and grants to higher education from such private donors as alumni, friends, corporations, foundations, and religious denominations (67 pages)

1) Keyword Reference:	Accessibility
2) Author:	Kimball, Lindsley F.
3) Author's Profession:	Foundation Staff
4) Title of Work:	"Guidelines on Grantmaking"
5) Type of Work:	Experiential Commentary
6) Name of Journal:	*Foundation News*
7) Publisher:	Council on Foundations
8) Date of Publication:	March/April 1974
9) Page(s):	24

Elements of the record layout established comparability among the studies on the following factors:

1) *Keyword Reference*: Enabled themes, words, and topics identified during content analysis to be recorded, sorted, and itemized, thereby citing evidence of their recurrence;

2) *Author's Profession*: Enabled the studies to be compared by the professions of their authors, thereby identifying works by "acknowledged experts" (Light and Pillemer 1984);

3) *Type of Work*: Enabled the studies to be distinguished as survey research, experiential commentary, analysis, or statistical or reference;

4) *Date of Publication*: Enabled the works to be compared by age, thereby allowing the lineage of recurring themes to be traced; and

5) *Name of Journal*: Enabled the works to be compared by the types of publications in which they appear, thereby distinguishing works in the expert literature from works in the popular literature.

Convergence of Themes

Having established variables to compare works in the study and keyword references to describe themes in the literature, a review of qualitative data next achieves "convergence" among themes (Guba 1978). Patton (1980) explains that convergence is the process of "figuring out what things fit together."

Themes in the literature are converged using two criteria, internal and external homogeneity (Guba 1978). Internal homogeneity is the extent to which themes belong in a certain category, while external homogeneity is the extent to which differences between categories are clear. Viewed internally, categories should be consistent and discrete. Viewed externally, categories should reflect the "whole picture" of the phenomenon under study (Patton 1980). One indication of weak external homogeneity is a large number of "unassignable or overlapping data items," indicating that the classification system lacks clarity or completeness.

Themes in the literature are evaluated for their salience and credibility (Patton 1980). Salient themes reflect issues that are germane, rather than secondary, while themes may be considered credible if discussed by multiple authors over long periods of time. Verifying the salience and credibility of themes is an "intuitive" process, according to Guba (1978), and "no infallible procedure exists for performing it." Researchers, therefore, must examine the "weight" of themes to verify their salience and credibility, navigating between the extremes of "hypercriticalness and hypocriticalness" (Feldman 1971). A hypercritical assessment of qualitative data would reject all themes on the grounds that they are merely the opinions of individuals quoted in the study. On the other hand, a hypocritical judgement of qualitative data would accept all statements as equally germane and credible. To avoid hypercriticalness and hypocriticalness, "justice must be tempered with mercy, but mercy must also be tempered with justice," for in the integration of themes, "certainty must be balanced with uncertainty" (Feldman 1971).

Themes which satisfy the criteria of salience and credibility, however, do not inevitably represent truth. Rather, the objective of a review of qualitative data is not necessarily to establish truth, but rather, to create "perspective" of the phenomenon under study (Patton 1980). Individuals who hypercritically judge reviews of qualitative data may consider such works subjective and unreliable. Also, many quantitative analysts believe that unless data can be expressed numerically, their validity cannot be tested. Patton (1980), however, indicates that "numbers do not protect against bias; they merely disguise it."

Although the quantitative paradigm has traditionally been considered the strongest research method, Patton (1980) believes that the model is "no longer so ominous." Moreover, Campbell and Cronbach, major spokesmen for quantitative research, have advocated qualitative methods (Campbell 1974; Cronbach 1975). "When two of the leading scholars of measurement and experimental design . . . strongly support qualitative studies, that is strong endorsement indeed" (House 1977). The goal of a review of qualitative data, therefore, is to achieve "qualitative objectivity" (Scriven 1972), and the goal of the qualitative researcher is to be factual, rather than distant from the phenomenon under study. "Distance does not guarantee objectivity," concludes Patton (1980); "it merely guarantees distance."

REVIEW OF THE LITERATURE

"Any study, or set of studies, benefits when put into the perspective . . . of other relevant studies."

Kenneth A. Feldman
"Using the Work of Others"
Sociology of Education (1971)

Mapping the Literature

This section examines the publication and thematic dimensions of the literature on foundations. The publication dimension includes the number, age, authors, and types of works in the study, while the thematic dimension identifies major issues in the literature on foundations.

One of the first steps in a review of qualitative data is selecting the literature to be synthesized. Feldman (1971) indicates that sampling a literature often begins by reviewing other reviews and integrations of the literature. However, in the 2,500 works synthesized for this study, no reviews of the literature on foundations were discovered, with the exception of O'Connell's 1983 work, *America's Voluntary Spirit,* which is a compendium of readings on philanthropy and voluntarism. The lack of reviews of the literature on foundations may be related to the general lack of information on foundations, a problem on which scholars have commented for at least the past fifty years. Chapter One cited the commentary on the shallowness of the literature on foundations by Lester (1935); Hollis (1938); the United States House of Representatives (1952); Andrews (1954); Kiger (1954); Macdonald (1956); Dickinson (1973); Rockefeller (1973); Cheit and Lobman (1979); Broce (1981); Boris (1985); Marchese, Bernstein, and Newman (1985); Nielsen (1985); Payton (1985); Sleeper (1985); Plinio (1986); and Read (Desruisseaux 1986e).

Number and Age of Works

The study contains citations from 428 works which were coded by year of publication to examine periods of publication. As shown on Table 17, the literature on foundations is modern, for nearly 90 percent of the works in the study were published after 1950.

The predominance of recent works in the literature may be attributable to two factors. First, in 1952, a major Congressional investigation disclosed abuses by foundations and generated increased dialogue in the philanthropic community. Among the major studies published shortly after this inquiry are *Attitudes Toward Giving* (Andrews 1953); *Public Accountability of Foundations and Charitable Trusts* (Russell Sage Foundation 1953); *Operating Principles of the Larger Foundations* (Kiger 1954); *Philanthropic Foundations* (Andrews 1956); *The Ford Foundation: The Men and the Millions* (Macdonald 1956); *Foundations: Twenty Viewpoints (Andrews, ed. 1965); and U.S. Philanthropic Foundations* (Weaver 1967).

A second reason for the number of recent works in the literature may be the Tax Reform Act of 1969. This law subjected foundations to taxation for the first time in American history, generating increased discussion of foundations in both the philanthropic and grantseeking communities. Some of the major works published in

Table 17

Publication Years of Works in the Study		
Decade	Number of Works	Percent of Total Works
Pre-1900	5	1.1
1900 to 1909	4	0.9
1910 to 1919	4	0.9
1920 to 1929	9	2.1
1930 to 1939	17	4.0
1940 to 1949	8	1.9
1950 to 1959	25	5.8
1960 to 1969	55	12.9
1970 to 1979	115	26.9
1980 to 1986	186	43.5
Totals	428	100.0
Publication Periods:		
1950 to 1986	381	89.0
1970 to 1986	301	70.3
Decade Increases:		
1950s over 1940s	17	212.5
1960s over 1950s	30	120.0
1970s over 1960s	60	109.1
1980s over 1970s	71	61.7

the wake of the Tax Reform Act of 1969 are *Private Giving and Public Policy* (Commission on Foundations and Private Philanthropy 1970); *Foundations Under Fire* (Reeves, ed. 1970); *Foundations: Their Use and Abuse* (Rudy 1970); "The Case Against Foundations" (Branch 1971); *The Money Givers* (Goulden 1971); *Giving and Taking* (Russell 1971); *The Big Foundations* (Nielsen 1972); *The Management of American Foundations* (Zurcher 1972); *The Foundation Administrator* (Zurcher and Dustan 1972); *Some General Principles and Guidelines for Grant-Making Foundations* (Council on Foundations 1973b); *The Philanthropoids* (Whitaker 1974); *Giving in America* (Commission on Private Philanthropy and Public Needs 1975); *Private Philanthropy: Report and Recommendations* (Donee Group 1976); and *Trustees and the Future of Foundations* (Nason 1977).

Types of Works

During content analysis, works were classified by four types: 1) survey research; 2) expert commentary; 3) analysis; and 4) statistical or reference. Works of survey research cite findings derived from questionnaires or interviews. Among the works of survey research in the study are *Wealth and Culture* (Lindeman 1936); *The Foundation Administrator* (Zurcher and Dustan 1972); "Criteria Grantors Use in Assessing Proposals" (Townsend 1974); "An Interview with John May" (Kennedy 1977); "Council Survey Highlights Foundation Staffing" (Boris and Unkle 1981); "What We Have Learned" (Boris 1984); and *Working in Foundations* (Odendahl, Boris, and Daniels 1985).

Works of expert commentary contain primarily the observations of foundation professionals, rather than conclusions derived from either survey or analytical research. Examples of works of expert commentary in the study are *The Gospel of Wealth and Other Timely Essays* (Carnegie 1900); "The Difficult Art of Giving" (Rockefeller 1908); "A Science of Giving" (Pritchett 1922); "Principles of Public Giving" (Rosenwald 1929); "Thoughts on Philanthropy and Philanthropoids" (Weaver 1965); "How Foundations Evaluate Requests" (Allen 1965); "Do We Know What We Are Doing?" (Brim 1973); "Understanding and Increasing Foundation Support" (Broce 1981); and *Speaking Out* (Pifer 1984b).

Works of analysis are more detailed investigations of foundations than are works of expert commentary. Among the works of analysis in the study are *Philanthropic Foundations and Higher Education* (Hollis 1938); *Operating Principles of the Larger Foundations* (Kiger 1954); *Philanthropy in the Shaping of American Higher Education* (Curti and Nash 1965); *Private Giving and Public Policy* (Commission on Foundations and Private Philanthropy 1970); *The Big Foundations* (Nielsen 1972); *The Philanthropoids* (Whitaker 1974); and *The Golden Donors* (Nielsen 1985).

Statistical or reference works present quantitative data or contain listings of foundations or grantees. Examples of statistical or reference publications in the study are *1984–85 Fact Book on Higher Education* (American Council on Education 1984); *Foundation Directory* (The Foundation Center 1985); *Voluntary Support of Education: 1984–85* (Council for Financial Aid to Education 1986); and *Financial Statistics of Institutions of Higher Education* (National Center for Education Statistics, selected years).

As shown on Table 18, nearly 54 percent of the works in the study are classified as expert commentary. One-third of the works are categorized as analytical, while nearly 8 pecent are survey

Table 18

Type of Works in the Study

Type	Number of Works	Percent of Total Works
Expert Commentary	230	53.7
Analysis	142	33.2
Survey Research	32	7.5
Statistical or Reference	24	5.6
Totals	428	100.0

research. Statistical or reference reports comprise the remaining 5 percent of works in the study.

The Professions of Authors

The professions of authors of works in the study were coded by eight occupational areas:

1) scholar: an independent authority or an expert associated with a university or institute who is neither a member of the foundation community nor a journalist, donee group official, or government officer. Among the authors classified as scholars are Cheit, Curti, Flexner, Nash, Nielsen, and Whitaker;

2) foundation association offical: an individual affiliated with an association which represents foundations. Examples of authors who are foundation association officials are Joseph and Boris of the Council on Foundations and Kurzig, an officer of the Foundation Center;

3) foundation founder: an original donor of a foundation; for example, Carnegie, Rockefeller, or Rosenwald;

4) foundation trustee: a member of the governing board of a foundation. Elliott, Freeman, Greenleaf, and Nason are among the authors in the study who are foundation trustees;

5) foundation staff: a member of the administrative or program staff of a foundation. Among the authors who are foundation staff are DeBakey, Pattillo, Payton, Pritchett, and Weaver;

6) donee group member: an individual serving an institution which is a foundation donee or grantseeker. Donee group members are often development officers or research directors of universities, museums, or social agencies. Among the authors in the study who are donee group members are Bothwell, Dickinson, Eisenberg, Landau, and Menninger;

Table 19

Professions of Authors of Works in the Study

Authors' Professions	Number of Authors	Percent of Total Authors
Foundation Staff	117	27.3
Scholars	109	25.5
Foundation Association Officials	82	19.2
Donee Group Members	46	10.8
Journalists	31	7.2
Foundation Trustees	20	4.7
Government Officials and Agencies	13	3.0
Foundation Founders	10	2.3
Total	428	100.0
By the Foundation Community: (Foundation Associations or Founders, Trustees, or Staff of Foundations)	229	53.5

7) journalist: an individual writing for a news or professional publication. Among the authors in the study who are journalists are Desruisseaux of *The Chronicle of Higher Education* and Teltsch and Tivnan of *The New York Times*.

8) government: an officer, agency, or branch of the federal, state, or local government. Among authors in the study from the government are Friedman, Marlowe, the National Center for Education Statistics, and the House of Representatives of the United States Congress.

The categories for the professions of authors are not mutually exclusive because some authors have held multiple professional posts. In such instances, the professions of an author were compared and the author was assigned the classification reflecting the most prominent or frequent profession. As shown on Table 19, nearly 54 percent of the authors in the study are members of the foundation community; namely, foundation association representatives or the founders, trustees, or staff members of foundations. Scholars comprise approximately 25 percent of the authors in the study, while members of the donee group constitute nearly 11 percent. Journalists and government officials or agencies comprise the remaining 10 percent of the authors in the study.

Themes in the Literature

The literature on foundations contains eight common themes relating to the internal and external environments of the organizations:

1) highlights or histories of individual foundations, landmark foundation programs, or recent foundation initiatives;
2) the quantitative dimension of foundations: their number, assets, grants, funding patterns, investment performance, and periods of establishment;
3) the personnel of foundations: the number, distribution, and compensation of foundation staff and trustees, as well as their educational, professional, and personal characteristics;
4) the accessibility of foundations, with some authors urging greater accessibility, while others question public accountability standards. The Foundation Center, the Council on Foundations, and many leading foundation spokesmen strongly advocate greater accessibility by foundations;
5) ethical issues, focusing on the interaction of foundations with donees during the evaluation of proposals and the monitoring of grant programs;
6) discussions on the grantmaking mission of foundations in response to manifold funding opportunities and the sometimes conflicting proposals of grantseekers, charters of donors, policies of trustees, initiatives of staff, programs of government, and needs of society. Responding perhaps to Bolling's 1978 call for "A Time for Reassessment," foundations are engaged in a reevaluation of mission, an activity which may be cyclical, for the reassessment of priorities by foundations was also noted by Curti and Nash (1965);
7) increased professionalism in foundations through the addition of staff or by cooperation between foundations in "Regional Associations of Grantmakers" (Foote 1986a). The need for improved research on all aspects of foundations is also discussed; and
8) ways to improve grantmaking effectiveness, with extensive discussion of the difficulty of wise grantmaking, the purposefulness of grantmaking, the importance of competent applicants, the necessity of feasible requests, the importance of clear writing in grant proposals, the importance of the continuity of grant programs, and the need for trust between grantor and grantee.

Literature Review Summary

The literature on foundations has grown significantly in size and substance in the last four decades. Nearly 90 percent of the works in the study were written after 1950, and over half the works in the study are classified as the commentary of officials of foundation associations or the founders, trustees, or staff members of foundations. The literature on foundations, therefore, is modern, professional, and perhaps most important, emerging.

III

FOUNDATIONS AND HIGHER EDUCATION

"The prosecution of fundamental researches will remain one of the major opportunities, perhaps the major opportunity, of the foundations, so long as they themselves endure."

Frederick P. Keppel
*The Foundation: Its Place in
American Life* (1930)

Purpose of the Chapter

This chapter examines the historical relationship of foundations and higher education, focusing on the financial contributions of foundations from 1920 to 1984; two landmark foundation programs, the General Education Board and the Carnegie Foundation for the Advancement of Teaching; and other major influences of foundations on the academy including educational research, women's colleges, and educational opportunities for blacks.

Historical Background

Higher education has been supported by philanthropy since its inauguration in the Western World. Plato's endowment of the Academy generated income until its dissolution almost 900 years later.

44

During the Middle Ages, gifts to Oxford and Cambridge established the college structure in universities, while John Harvard's bequest of 800 pounds and 400 books established this nation's first college (Curti and Nash 1965).

Few institutions in the United States bear the mark of philanthropy as noticeably as higher education. Hollis (1938) notes the "kinship" of foundations and higher education, and Keppel (1930), first President of the Carnegie Corporation, writes that the foundation's "nearest relative . . . without any question . . . is the university." Whitaker (1974) adds that foundations and higher education have "always been close," noting that observers have suggested that foundations "turn themselves into universities." Studies by the Council on Foundations show that foundation officers are often recruited from higher education and that foundations use faculty to evaluate grant programs. Curti and Nash (1965) consider philanthropy to be the "telling force" in higher education, and educational philanthropists have been cited for the "magnitude of their support and for the weight of their influence" (Cowley 1980).

The modern relationship of foundations and higher education begins in the early 20th century with Andrew Carnegie and John D. Rockefeller. These philanthropists each created approximately ten foundations, but Rockefeller's General Education Board and the Carnegie Foundation for the Advancement of Teaching may have had the greatest early impact on higher education. The General Education Board was founded in 1902 and, by its closing in 1960, had appropriated nearly $325 million for the "promotion of education in the United States" (Fosdick 1952). The Carnegie Foundation for the Advancement of Teaching was established in 1905 with an endowment of $10 million to provide pensions for American and Canadian professors. The Foundation continues today as a leader in educational research.

New Patterns of Philanthropy

Foundation philanthropy in the early 20th century differed in two important ways from previous patterns of giving (Curti and Nash 1965). First, the "mechanism of giving" changed, as grantmaking decisions "transferred from the philanthropist to the 'philanthropoid', an individual who made a career of giving the money of others" (Curti and Nash 1965). The second difference was that foundations departed from general support of institutions, directing their grants to reforms and experiments. The changes in early foundation philosophy were accompanied by a period of introspection in which foundations questioned "what (their) role should be in shaping higher education" (Curti and Nash 1965), an evaluation which may have been a forerunner to the current reassessment of mission by foundations.

Hollis (1938) identifies three policy periods of foundations in the early 20th century. The first period, which ended with World War I, saw foundations making grants to the "general endowment of colleges." The second period, ending in 1924, was one of grants for special purposes such as medical education, teachers' salaries, and "post-war emergencies." The third period, from 1925 to the late 1930s, saw foundations "directly (influencing) the quality of education by grants to specific projects."

Lindeman (1936) believes that most philanthropists had education in mind when they made their bequests, reflecting the American belief that education encourages social and economic advancement. Kiger (1954) indicates that education remained a major interest of philanthropists through the 1940s, and he attributes the emphasis to the "basic American philosophy of progress." Explains Kiger:

> Americans generally have an implicit faith that by study and learning the world will become a better and better place.... Both the men who founded and those who have guided the foundations shared this belief.... For by study and learning (philanthropists held that) many of the woes of mankind could be alleviated or eliminated right at the source, the mind of man itself (1954).

Early philanthropists usually selected the "strongest and most promising" higher education institutions to receive their support (Curti and Nash 1965). Indeed, between 1923 and 1939, about 86 percent of the $103 million granted to the academy by the five largest foundations went to only thirty-six colleges and universities (Curti and Nash 1965). Note the authors: "Out of a total of more than a thousand (higher education) institutions in the United States, this was indeed concentrated giving." Hollis, too, found that foundations favored a minority of institutions, noting in 1940 that twenty schools received 73 percent of foundation funds, and "some eight hundred colleges got nothing." Summarizing the early impact of foundations on the academy, Hollis (1940) termed foundations the "most influential of the external agencies that have modified higher education as a process or institution."

The Carnegie Corporation

One of the first leading educational foundations was the Carnegie Corporation of New York. A foundation despite its name, the Corporation was founded in 1911 with $25 million to "promote the advancement and diffusion of knowledge and understanding." In 1912, Carnegie's second gift of $100 million "swelled (the foundation's) resources" and, with the election of President Keppel in 1922, the Corporation entered new areas such as food research, the study of atomic structure, and research on engineering and aerodynamics (Curti and Nash 1965). Joining forces with other foundations, the Corporation supported experimental colleges, and by 1938, had granted more than $5 million for progressive institutions such as Bennington, Antioch, Bard, Stephens, Southwestern, and Teachers College at Columbia University (Curti and Nash 1965). In 1947, President Devereux C. Josephs affirmed the Corporation's support of innovative ideas, writing, "There is small probability that grants will be made for endowment, for buildings, for equipment, or for the current support of established enterprises."

The Ford Foundation

Another early leading grantmaker was the Ford Foundation, established by Henry Ford and his son Edsel in 1936. The Fords, who had refused to extend ownership of the Motor Company beyond their immediate family, perceived new tax laws as an end to family control because the laws required selling a large portion of the Ford stock to outsiders (Curti and Nash 1965). Hurried consultation with the Company's lawyers produced a solution. A foundation would be established to which the Fords could bequeath their stock. By the deaths of Edsel Ford in 1943 and his father four years later, the Foundation had received 90 percent of the Ford Motor Company stock with an estimated value of $2 billion.

Hoffman and Hutchins, the first President and Vice President of the Ford Foundation, made two initial recommendations: 1) higher education would be supported as a "basic tool in the solution of mankind's problems;" and 2) "novel, experimental programs would be favored" (Curti and Nash 1965). To distribute educational grants, the Foundation created the Fund for the Advancement of Education, which in 1959 spent more than $14 million on teacher training, while the Ford Foundation itself awarded $210 million to increase faculty salaries at over 600 liberal arts colleges. Another $50 million in Ford grants went to 126 institutions which had independently tried to increase faculty wages. From 1950 to 1959, the Ford Foundation made grants of nearly $750 million to all levels of education, contributions which were unparalleled in American philanthropy.

Table 20

Foundation Grants to Education, 1921 to 1930 (Millions)			
	1921	1930	1921–1930
Grants to	$15.0	$32.6	$223.0
Education	41.3%	52.8%	43.0%
Grants by All Foundations	$36.3	$61.7	$518.4

Source: *Wealth and Culture*, Lindeman (1936)

Financial Contributions of Foundations to Education: 1921 to 1930

Foundations have been a leading donor to education from at least 1920. From 1921 through 1930, Lindeman (1936) found that all forms of education received 43 percent of the grants of the 100 largest foundations. As shown on Table 20, education received over $15 million, or 41 percent of the $36 million awarded in 1921. Health, the second largest recipient in 1921, received 33 percent of foundation funds. In 1930, education again received the largest share of foundation funds, nearly 53 percent of the $61.7 million awarded. Early grants to education heavily favored higher education. As shown on Table 21, from 1921 to 1930, over 60 pecent of foundation grants to education went to higher education.

Financial Contributions of Foundations to Education: 1961 to 1984

The Foundation Center has reported foundation grantmaking since the early 1960s, and from 1961 to 1984, education was the leading recipient of foundation funds. In 1961, as shown on Table 22, education received over $100 million from foundations, outpacing health, the second leading recipient, by 57 percent.

In 1970, as shown on Table 23, education remained the leading recipient of foundation funds, garnering 36 percent of total grants and outdistancing welfare, the second leading recipient, by over 106 percent.

From 1961 through 1970, education received over $1.8 billion from foundations, or 32 percent of all foundation grants. The second leading recipient was international activities, which garnered $850 million, or 15 percent of all foundation funds. From 1961 through 1970, therefore, education received double the foundation grants of the next closest grantee. Lewis (1971) notes that in "all ten

Table 21

Foundation Grants to Higher Education as a Share of Foundation Grants to Education, 1921 to 1930 (Millions)

Type of Education	Grants	Percent of Grants to Education
Higher Education	$135.9	60.9
Elementary and Secondary Education	32.9	14.8
Unclassified	11.5	5.2
Adult Education	9.2	4.1
Libraries	7.5	3.4
Vocational Education	6.1	2.7
Aesthetic and Cultural Education	5.8	2.6
Elementary (a) Education	5.8	2.6
Secondary (a) Education	3.9	1.8
Publications	2.9	1.3
Leadership Training	1.2	.1
Conferences	.2	—
Pre-School Education	.1	—
Total	$223.0	100.0

(a) Grants were made to institutions offering both elementary and secondary education, and Lindeman (1936) found "no way of separating the two items."

Source: *Wealth and Culture*, Lindeman 1936

Table 22

Leading Fields of Interest of Foundations, 1961 (Millions)

Field	Rank in 1961	1961 Grants Received Amount	Percent of Total
Education	1	$107	31
Health	2	68	19
International Activities	3	62	17
Welfare	4	43	12
Sciences	5	37	11
Humanities	6	25	7
Religion	7	9	3
Totals		$351	100

Source: The Foundation Center, *Foundation Directory* (1971)

Table 23

Leading Fields of Interest of Foundations, 1970 (Millions)

Field	Rank in 1970	1970 Grants Received	
		Amount	Percent of Total
Education	1	$281	36
Welfare	2	136	17
Health	3	121	15
Sciences	4	93	12
International Activities	5	59	7
Humanities	6	52	7
Religion	7	51	6
Totals		$793	100

Source: The Foundation Center, *Foundation Directory* (1971)

years" of the 1960s, "Education was the most favored field, its proportion ranging from 24 to 46 percent, and averaging out at 32, or very nearly a third of foundation dollars." Moreover, adds Lewis (1971), education's share of foundation funds was probably even greater because a "substantial amount" of the funds to international activities, sciences, and humanities were channeled through educational institutions. Indeed, reports Lewis (1971), "probably more than half of all foundation dollars went to Education broadly defined."

From 1970 through 1979, education continued to receive the largest portion of foundation dollars, although its share fell from 36 percent in 1970 to approximately 25 percent in 1979. In 1980, how-

Table 24

Leading Fields of Interest of Foundations, 1980 (Millions)

Field	Rank in 1980	1980 Grants Received	
		Amount	Percent of Total
Health	1	$ 299	25
Welfare	2	292	25
Education	3	266	22
Humanities	4	161	14
Sciences	5	75	6
Social Science (a)	6	68	6
Religion	7	29	2
Totals		$1,190	100

(a) In 1980, Social Science was added as a field of interest replacing International Activities.

Source: The Foundation Center, *Foundation Directory,* selected years

Table 25

Leading Fields of Interest of Foundations, 1984 (Millions)

Field	Rank in 1984	1984 Grants Received	
		Amount	Percent of Total
Welfare	1	$ 454	28
Health	2	390	24
Education	3	286	17
Humanities	4	229	14
Social Science	5	126	8
Sciences	6	123	7
Religion	7	38	2
Totals		$1,646	100

Source: The Foundation Center, *Foundation Directory,* selected years

ever, as shown on Table 24, education fell to third among the seven fields of interest, as health acquired 25 percent of foundation grants, welfare 24 percent, and education 22 percent.

In 1984, education continued to rank third among the seven fields of interest, receiving grants of $286 million, or 17 percent of all foundation awards. As shown on Table 25, welfare received the most foundation funds in 1984, while health ranked second.

Lindeman's 1936 discovery that over 60 percent of foundation grants for education in the 1920s went to higher education is mirrored by the findings of modern scholars. Cheit and Lobman (1979) report that a survey by the National Planning Association found that 78 percent of grants for education were for higher education and that foundation awards to humanities, sciences, and health "also contain grants for education." Add Cheit and Lobman (1979):

> Sixty-eight pecent of the grants for 'science and science-related activities' went to colleges and universities (while) over one-third of the expenditures for 'health and health-related activities' were for research and manpower training, much of which, we assume, took place at universities. It also seems safe to assume that a substantial portion of humanities and international activities funds were for higher education.

Financial Contributions' Summary

Education, and particularly higher education, has been a leading recipient of foundation funds since 1920. Lindeman (1936) reports that during the 1920s, education received 43 percent of foundation funds and ranked first among seven fields of interest. Lindeman (1936) also reports that in the 1920s, higher education received over 60 percent of foundation grants to education, outpacing its nearest competitor, elementary and secondary education, by 219 percent. From 1961 through 1979, education was the leading recipient of foundation funds, garnering over 31 percent of all foundation grants. In 1980, however, education slipped to third place among the seven fields of interest where it remained through 1984. Notwithstanding its recent decline in share, education, especially higher education, continues to receive a substantial portion of foundation funds, confirming its position as a leading field of interest of foundations since at least 1920.

Landmark Foundation Programs: The General Education Board

In 1902, with a grant of $1 million, Rockefeller created the General Education Board to "promote education in the United States without distinction of sex, race, or creed" (*General Education Board* 1915). Rockefeller had three main motives for establishing the Board. First, the foundation was designed to "bring order and efficiency" to Rockefeller's philanthropy, which had become too large for his own office and that of the American Baptist Education Society, original manager of his charity (Curti and Nash 1965). Second, the Board was created to demonstrate Rockefeller's belief that capitalism, not socialism, was capable of promoting the greatest "general good" (Rockefeller 1909). Third, the General Education Board was founded to improve education in the South.

In 1901, Rockefeller's son attended a conference in North Carolina on education problems in the South. "Deeply moved by the plight of the Southerner," he convinced his father to extend the Rockefeller philanthropies in that direction (Curti and Nash 1965). A five-member board was assembled, which included Gilman, President of the University of California and later Johns Hopkins University, and Gates, an official of the American Baptist Education Society. In 1905, the General Education Board received $10 million from Rockefeller to "promote a comprehensive system of higher education in the United States" (*General Education Board* 1915). Over the next 15 years, Rockefeller gave the Board nearly $120 million, enabling the foundation to "exert a considerable influence on American colleges and universities" (Curti and Nash 1965).

One of the Board's first acts was a survey of higher education institutions, which concluded that the nation had an "overabundance of colleges," many with neither the income nor the equipment to function "passably well" (Curti and Nash 1965). In Ohio, which then had a population of 4.7 million, the Board identified over 40 "so-called colleges and universities," almost twice as many as the

German nation whose population was nearly 65 million. The Board held that "institutions in such numbers cannot be supported, cannot be manned, (and) cannot procure qualified students" (*General Education Board* 1915). What was lacking in Amercian higher education, the Board believed, was a "general design" that would bring "order to the chaos" (*General Education Board* 1915).

Although the Board intended to put "no pressure, direct or indirect" on colleges, the Board considered its funds best invested in institutions which were "comfortable financially" (*General Education Board* 1915). "Coercion may not have been overt," report Curti and Nash (1965), "but in making grants the board naturally selected those institutions whose policies . . . they approved." Accordingly, because colleges were attracted by the Board's funds, the foundation's grantmaking criteria became "unofficial standards" for many institutions (Curti and Nash 1965). In choosing colleges for support, the Board relied on the principle of "optimum location" (Curti and Nash 1965), selecting institutions in "populous and wealthy" areas where enrollment might best be maintained and where prospective donors could help ensure financial stability. Colleges in the "hinterland," explain Curti and Nash (1965), had "poorer chances" to receive the Board's support. To illustrate its "laws of college growth," the Board prepared a series of maps showing its choices of the best locations for colleges (*General Education Board* 1915).

In 1925, the Board awarded nearly $60 million in endowment grants based largely on the "promise" of institutions (Fosdick 1952). The Board looked unkindly on colleges which "begged" for a grant and which claimed that they would be "obliged to close without it" (Curti and Nash 1965). Thus, the Board restricted its grants to established colleges and universities, and by 1920, nearly 75 percent of the Board's gifts had gone to only twenty institutions (Brubacher and Rudy 1958). In 1926, the Board shifted from making endowment grants, partly because the demand for such awards exceeded its resources (General Education Board, *Annual Report, 1925–26*). Rather, the Board directed its attention to medical education following the recommendations of Flexner's landmark report, *Medical Education in the United States and Canada* (1910), which recommended abolition of all but 31 of the nation's 155 medical schools. Using Johns Hopkins University as a model for medical education, the Board in 1913 awarded the University $1.5 million to pay faculty full-time salaries to eliminate part-time instructors. The Board believed that medical education was important enough to require full-time faculty, a position strongly recommended by Flexner (1910). Between 1919 and 1921, Rockefeller gave the Board an additional $45 million for medical education, and the Rockefeller

Foundation added other funds for the new priority. "Besides the gift to Hopkins," report Curti and Nash (1965), "millions were given to Yale, Washington University in St. Louis, the University of Chicago, and Vanderbilt," for the Board believed that such grants would "oblige the remainder of the nation's medical schools to either raise their standards or close." By 1929, when the Board curtailed its support of medical education, "America's medical schools had been reduced in number and so improved as to place them among the world's finest" (Flexner 1952).

Landmark Foundation Programs: The Carnegie Foundation for the Advancement of Teaching

Like Rockefeller, Carnegie began the 20th century with considerable surplus wealth. He believed that philanthropy should be constructive, and that the wealthy should in their lifetimes donate all but what was needed to provide reasonably for their families. Wrote Carnegie (1889): "The man who dies thus rich dies disgraced."

In 1904, Carnegie received a proposal from Pritchett, President of the Massachusetts Institute of Technology, to provide retirement pensions for the Institute's faculty. Carnegie had long recognized the problem, for as a new trustee of Cornell University in 1890, he had been astonished to learn that professors were paid less than many of his clerks (Carnegie 1920). Intrigued by the idea of faculty pensions at one institution, Carnegie asked Pritchett to investigate the need at all colleges and universities. Pritchett's report estimated that retirement pensions for faculty in 92 institutions could be provided with the income from a gift of $10 million. Carnegie donated that amount to provide "retiring pensions for the teachers of universities, colleges, and technical schools in our country, Canada and Newfoundland," noting that "expert calculation shows that the revenue will be ample for the purpose." To direct the distribution of pensions, Carnegie created the Foundation for the Advancement of Teaching, and Pritchett resigned from the Massachusetts Institute of Technology to become the Foundation's first President.

Pritchett immediately recognized the possibility of resolving the "confusion that existed in American higher education," believing that by developing consistent admission standards, "one of the most glaring defects" in higher education could be corrected (Curti and Nash 1965). Joining Pritchett as trustees of the Carnegie Foundation were Eliot and Butler, educators who would use the Foundation to "accelerate a campaign in which (they) had long been engaged . . . upgrading American secondary and higher education" (Cowley 1980). Eliot, former President of Harvard University, had been tackling the problem since 1879 when he convinced most New England colleges to adopt uniform admission criteria in the study of English (Cowley 1980). Eliot had also been the "prime force" behind the National Education Association's Committee of Ten on Secondary School Studies which he chaired and whose members Butler nominated (Butler 1893). This committee was one of the "most productive in the history of American education," setting the academic world "on fire with its desire to improve secondary education" (Cowley 1980).

The Carnegie Foundation insisted that colleges receiving its pensions restrict admission to students with four years of secondary education. To explain the requirement, the Foundation hosted a conference in 1908 in which the "Carnegie unit" was introduced as a "measuring device" of fifteen units of secondary work (Curti and Nash 1965). Hechinger (1967) explains that Carnegie units were the "qualitative yardsticks" of a curriculum, and that the units were adopted as the "measurable ingredients of a student's course work or of a teacher's classroom functions." The Carnegie Foundation also sought to define a college, a task made difficult by the proliferation of institutions. Macdonald (1956) explains that "in handing out pensions . . . the question naturally arose: What *is* a college? Even Carnegie didn't aspire to, or want to, take care of the myriad 'diploma mills' and tiny backwoods religious 'colleges.' " The Foundation insisted that institutions receiving Carnegie pensions have: 1) at least six professors with doctorates, which usually meant a corresponding number of academic departments; 2) a four-year curriculum for the bachelor's degree; 3) an admissions requirement of four years of secondary education; and 4) an endowment of $200,000. Although the standards may seem "ridiculously meager today," only a "small proportion" of the colleges and universities at that time could satisfy them (Cowley 1980). Indeed, of the approximately 500 higher education institutions in the United States in 1905, only about 160 had annual incomes of $50,000 or more. Thus, the Foundation could initially find only approximately 50 private, nondenominational institutions meeting its four criteria.

The Foundation believed that the weakest colleges and universities were denominational institutions whose sectarianism "prevented adequate growth and support from a diverse public" (Curti and Nash 1965). Accordingly, the Foundation awarded no pension grants to denominational colleges. However, responding to the policy "for weal or for woe," a dozen church-related colleges including

Bowdoin, Dickinson, Swarthmore, and Wesleyan "swiftly dropped their church connections" (Cowley 1980).

Despite the positive effects of the Carnegie pensions, the Foundation was criticized for its effort to reshape higher education and control the nation's universities (Candler 1909). Faculty members themselves attacked the pensions, claiming that salary increases were more important than pensions and that faculty had little control over the Foundation (Cattell 1919). Other critics charged that the Foundation sought to standardize higher education, protesting that its policies failed to recognize the diversity of institutions. Public universities, which had been omitted from the pensions by Pritchett, appealed so vigorously that Carnegie countered Pritchett's policy and awarded $5 million in 1908 for faculty in public institutions. In his report, *A Comprehensive Plan of Insurance and Annuities for College Teachers* (1916), Pritchett admitted the inadequacies of using the pension system to reconstruct American higher education. Two years later, the pension program of the Carnegie Foundation was committed beyond its resources and was reorganized into the Teachers Insurance and Annuity Association, dropping the previously enforced admission standards and requiring that faculty contribute 5 percent of their salaries to participate. Today, the Teachers Insurance and Annuity Association is one of the largest retirement programs in the nation, and the curriculum standards developed by the Carnegie Foundation continue to be used in secondary education.

Other Influences of Foundations in Higher Education

In addition to the landmark foundation programs, foundations have made many other advances in higher education. Cowley (1980) contends that a "large share of the credit" for the progress of colleges and universities belongs to foundations, noting that foundations have "directly or indirectly altered the policies of every American college and university."

Educational research and the accessibility of higher education to women and blacks are two major contributions of foundations to the academy. Hechinger (1967) cites other programs in which foundations were instrumental.

> Who but a foundation . . . would offer funds for experiments to predict students' artistic ability? Who would attempt to find out objectively the effects of parochial school education on American Catholics? How would it be possible . . . to test the effectiveness of . . . new pedagogical approaches (to) the teaching of reading . . . ?

The "principal importance" of foundation philanthropy, however, may have been establishing research centers in colleges and universities (Curti and Nash 1965). Conclude the authors: "For better or for worse, the millions of dollars of foundation philanthropy have encouraged a gradual redefinition of the role of the professor (in) American higher education" (1965).

Foundations have also been instrumental in the education of women. In the mid-19th century, many colleges and universities "threw up a solid barrier of opposition" to the admission of women. Philanthropists, however, believed that women should be entitled to the same education as men. Philanthropy, therefore, was used to "circumvent established interests," and such institutions as Vassar, Smith, Wellesley, and Bryn Mawr "(owe) their existence" to foundations (Curti and Nash 1965). Although the government and higher education institutions later encouraged the education of women, philanthropy "greatly speeded (its) development" (Curti and Nash 1965).

Foundations have supported the education of blacks since the Peabody Education Fund was established in 1867. The General Education Board, between 1902 and 1960, made grants of over $40 million to historically black colleges, while the Carnegie Foundation for the Advancement of Teaching also made the education of blacks a priority. The Phelps-Stokes Fund and the Julius Rosenwald Fund chose the education of blacks as a "special domain," with the latter foundation contributing over $20 million to black colleges by 1948 (Hechinger 1967). Other foundations joined the effort to expand the accessibility of higher education to blacks. The Ford, Sloan, Danforth, Rockefeller, and Carnegie foundations made sizeable grants to historically black colleges. The Carnegie Corporation established links between black colleges and predominently white institutions, creating partnerships between Brown University and the Tougaloo Southern Christian College, the University of Michigan and the Tuskegee Institute, and Cornell and Yale with the Hampton Institute. Conclude Curti and Nash (1965): "Philanthropy . . . financed the extension of higher education to the Negro (and foundations poured) millions into Negro colleges, which in time developed a strength and reputation considerably greater than the segregated institutions that the states supported."

Summary: Foundations and Higher Education

Foundations and higher education have enjoyed a long partnership of mission and finance. Academic programs have been developed through the generosity of foundations with particular interests. Buildings and equipment have been added, courses and credits have been established, admission and degree standards have been founded, salaries have been increased, and research has been encouraged. "Again and again in the history of American higher education," conclude Curti and Nash (1965), foundations have been at the "cutting edge of new ideas."

IV

DIMENSIONS OF FOUNDATIONS: QUANTITATIVE, ACCESSIBILITY, AND PERSONNEL

Purpose of the Chapter

This chapter presents the quantitative, accessibility, and personnel dimensions of foundations to provide a basic description of the organizations. The quantitative dimension includes the number, types, assets, and grants of foundations, as well as their geographic distribution, periods of establishment, and funding trends. The accessibility dimension cites the record of communication by foundations with grantseekers, the federal government, and the general public. The history of foundations publishing annual reports and listing descriptive data in the *Foundation Directory* is also provided. The personnel dimension presents the personal, educational, and professional characteristics of the staff members of foundations. The findings of longitudinal and point-in-time studies of foundation staff are cited, and a summary of the characteristics of foundation trustees is offered.

THE QUANTITATIVE DIMENSION

Definition of a Foundation

The Foundation Center, which publishes the *Foundation Directory*, defines a foundation as a

Table 26

Number, Assets, and Grants of Foundations in the 1985 *Foundation Directory* (Assets and Grants in Millions)

Foundation Type	Number	Percent of Total	Assets	Percent of Total	Grants	Percent of Total
Independent	3,466	78.7	$52,712	83.6	$2,898	71.0
Company	723	16.4	2,995	4.7	803	19.7
Community	134	3.1	2,773	4.4	242	5.9
Operating	79	1.8	4,594	7.3	137	3.4
Total	4,402	100.0	$63,074	100.0	$4,080	100.0

Source: The Foundation Center (1985)

> nongovernmental, nonprofit organization with its own funds (and) program managed by its own trustees and directors, which was established to maintain or aid educational, social, charitable, religious, or other activities serving the common welfare primarily by making grants to other nonprofit organizations (1985).

Although the *Foundation Directory* (1985) lists only 4,402 foundations, or 19 percent of the nation's estimated 23,000 foundations, the grantmakers in the sourcebook held 97 percent of the assets of all foundations and made 85 percent of all foundation grants in 1983, the base year of the *Directory*. Assets of foundations in the 1985 *Directory* totalled $63.1 billion, while their grants were $4.1 billion.

In the *Directory,* the Foundation Center includes only foundations which meet its definition and which have assets of at least $1 million or make annual grants of at least $100,000. The Foundation Center excludes four types of foundations from the *Directory:* 1) foundations whose grantmaking is restricted to specified organizations; 2) foundations which function as endowments for special purposes within parent institutions (such as college foundations); 3) operating foundations without active grantmaking programs; and 4) foundations which make appeals to the general public for funds.

Types of Foundations

The Foundation Center lists four types of foundations: independent, company-sponsored, community, and operating. An independent foundation is commonly known as a private foundation and is the most prominent foundation type in number, assets, and grants. Of the 4,402 foundations in the 1985 *Foundation Directory,* 3,466, or 79 percent, are independent foundations. Of the $63.1 billion in assets held by the *Directory* foundations, $52.7 billion, or 84 per-

Table 27

The Ten Largest Foundations, by Assets, 1983 or 1984 (Millions)

Foundation	Assets	Effective Date
Ford Foundation	$3,498	September 30, 1984
J. Paul Getty Trust	2,684	September 30, 1984
MacArthur Foundation	1,920	December 31, 1983
W. K. Kellogg Foundation	1,292	August 31, 1984
Robert Wood Johnson Foundation	1,174	December 31, 1984
Pew Memorial Trust	1,171	December 31, 1983
Rockefeller Foundation	1,102	December 31, 1984
Andrew W. Mellon Foundation	1,017	December 31, 1984
Lilly Endowment	889	December 31, 1984
Kresge Foundation	$ 814	December 31, 1984

Source: The Foundation Center (1985)

cent, are held by independent foundations. In 1983, independent foundations made grants of nearly $2.9 billion, or 71 percent of the $4.1 billion awarded by all foundations.

A company-sponsored foundation derives its funds from a profit-making concern, but is "independently constituted" to make grants, although "not without regard for the business interests of the corporation" (The Foundation Center 1985). In 1983, company-sponsored foundations numbered 723, or 16 percent of all foundations. Their assets totalled nearly $3 billion, or 5 percent of the assets of all foundations. Grants of company-sponsored foundations totalled over $800 million, or nearly 20 percent of all foundation awards.

Table 28

The Ten Largest Company-Sponsored Foundations, by Assets, 1983 or 1984 (Millions)

Foundation	Assets	Effective Date
Alcoa Foundation	$168	December 31, 1984
General Motors Foundation	123	December 31, 1984
AT&T Foundation	86	December 31, 1984
Amoco Foundation	76	December 31, 1984
Exxon Education Foundation	60	December 31, 1983
General Electric Foundation	54	December 31, 1983
Shell Companies Foundation	48	December 31, 1983
Ford Motor Foundation	48	December 31, 1984
Mobil Foundation	20	December 31, 1984
Aetna Life and Casualty Foundation	$18	December 31, 1983

Source: The Foundation Center (1985)

Table 29

The Ten Largest Community Foundations, by Assets,
1983 or 1984 (Millions)

Foundation	Assets	Effective Date
San Francisco Foundation	$461	June 30, 1984
New York Community Trust	370	December 31, 1983
Cleveland Foundation	305	December 31, 1984
Chicago Community Trust	176	September 30, 1984
Boston Foundation	115	June 30, 1984
Communities Foundation of Texas	90	June 30, 1984
Hartford Foundation for Public Giving	78	September 30, 1984
Saint Paul Foundation	74	December 31, 1984
Pittsburgh Foundation	70	December 31, 1984
Columbus Foundation	$64	December 31, 1983

Source: The Foundation Center (1985)

A community foundation is much like an independent foundation, but its funds are derived from many donors, rather than a single source as is usually the case with independent foundations (The Foundation Center 1985). Grants by community foundations are often made to a specific locality or region, and their governing boards usually represent the geographic areas served. Of the 4,402 foundations in the 1985 *Foundation Directory*, 134, or 3.1 percent, are community foundations. Their assets in 1983 totalled nearly $2.8 billion, or 4.4 percent of all foundation holdings. Grants by community foundations were $242 million, or nearly 6 percent of all foundation awards.

An operating foundation, according to the Foundation Center (1985), is a private foundation whose primary purpose is to conduct "research, social welfare, or other programs." Although operating foundations may make grants, the sum of such awards is usually smaller than the funds expended on their own programs. Of the 4,402 foundations in the 1985 *Foundation Directory*, 79, or 1.8 percent, are operating foundations. The assets of operating foundations in 1983 totalled nearly $4.6 billion and represented 7.3 percent of the assets of all foundations. Grants by operating foundations totalled $137 million, or 3.4 percent of all foundation awards.

Assets and Grants of Foundations

According to the Foundation Center (1985), the assets of *Directory* foundations have doubled since 1972, with the largest increase, 32.7 percent, occurring from 1981 to 1983. Grants of *Directory*

Table 30

The Ten Largest Operating Foundations, by Assets, 1983 (a) (Millions)	
Foundation	Assets
J. Paul Getty Trust (b)	$2,384
Norton Simon Foundation	275
Robert A. Welch Foundation	181
Amherst H. Wilder Foundation	174
Norton Simon Art Foundation	159
Menil Foundation	93
Charles F. Kettering Foundation	87
Annie E. Casey Foundation	69
Russell Sage Foundation	67
Liberty Fund	$67

(a): Because the Foundation Center does not cite the effective dates of the assets of the ten largest operating foundations, the year 1983, the base year of the 1985 *Foundation Directory*, is used.

(b): The J. Paul Getty Trust was established in 1953 for the "primary purpose of operating an art museum" (The Foundation Center 1985). In 1982, the foundation received a gift of $1.2 billion from the estate of J. Paul Getty.

Source: The Foundation Center (1985)

foundations, as shown on Table 31, have risen by over 163 percent since 1972. The largest increase in grantmaking occurred from 1979 to 1981 when federal law required foundations to make annual grants of the "greater of adjusted net income or 5 percent of the market value of assets" (The Foundation Center 1985). The "payout" requirement was changed to 5 percent of the market value of assets, irrespective of income, by the Economic Recovery Tax Act of 1981. Although *Directory* foundations continue to make charitable

Table 31

Assets and Grants of *Directory* Foundations: 1972 to 1983 (Millions of Dollars)					
Base Year	Number of Foundations	Assets	Percent Increase (Decrease)	Grants	Percent Increase (Decrease)
1972	2,533	$31,510	—	$1,548	—
1975	2,818	28,635	(9.1)	1,808	16.5
1977	3,138	32,359	13.0	2,062	14.1
1979	3,363	38,553	19.1	2,483	20.4
1981	4,063	47,541	23.3	3,480	40.1
1983	4,402	$63,075	32.7	$4,081	17.3

Source: The Foundation Center (1985)

awards in excess of the required 5 percent of their assets, the 1981 legislation appears to have modified the rapid increases in foundation giving (The Foundation Center 1985).

Geographic Distribution of Foundations

As shown on Table 32, nearly half of the foundations in the *Foundation Directory* are located in eight states: Illinois, Indiana, Michigan, New Jersey, New York, Ohio, Pennsylvania, and Wisconsin. The Foundation Center (1985) attributes this concentration to "past economic and industrial development (and) the personal preferences of the founders."

Although eight states contain the most foundations, these states have recently experienced "much slower growth (in establishing new foundations) than (have) other regions" (The Foundation Center 1985). In 1975, for example, foundations in New Jersey, New York, and Pennsylvania held 47 percent of the assets and made 46 percent of the grants of all foundations in the *Directory*. In 1983, however, the assets and grants of foundations in these three states were 37 and 36 percent of those of all *Directory* foundations. While states in the Foundation Center's Mid-Atlantic region have experienced a decline in the number of new foundations, the South, Southwest, and Pacific regions have seen an increase in foundations because of "changing demographic patterns and relatively rapid economic industrial growth" (The Foundation Center 1985).

Patterns of Funding

Since 1980, The Foundation Center has monitored patterns of foundation funding by recording the grantees of a sample of 460 foundations. Although the sample represents only 2 percent of the nation's foundations, the grantmakers in the sample account for almost 40 percent of the total foundation grants awarded annually (The Foundation Center 1985).

The Foundation Center uses seven categories to monitor funding patterns: cultural activities, education, health, religion, science, social science, and welfare. As shown on Table 33, since 1980, foundations have placed strong emphasis on the general welfare category, which in 1984 received 27.5 percent of all foundation grants (The Foundation Center 1985). Giving to health programs remained fairly stable from 1980 through 1984, as health received nearly 23 percent of all foundation awards. Giving to education declined from 22 percent of all foundation grants in 1980 to 17 percent in 1984, despite an increase in 1982. Grants for cultural activities, according

Table 32

Geographic Distribution of Foundations in the *Foundation Directory* (1985), by Number and Assets (Millions of Dollars)

Region and States	Foundations		Assets	
	Number	Percent	Amount	Percent
Mid-Atlantic	1,226	27.9	$23,532	37.3
New Jersey	108		2,169	
New York	857		16,232	
Pennsylvania	261		5,131	
East North-Central	862	19.6	12,128	19.2
Illinois	278		4,090	
Indiana	64		1,403	
Michigan	143		3,870	
Ohio	273		2,122	
Wisconsin	104		642	
Pacific	488	11.1	9,329	14.8
Alaska	2		2	
California	371		8,385	
Hawaii	23		140	
Oregon	33		346	
Washington	59		455	
West South-Central	371	8.4	5,785	9.2
Arkansas	12		91	
Louisiana	37		197	
Oklahoma	58		1,165	
Texas	264		4,333	
South Atlantic	539	12.2	4,961	7.9
Delaware	38		447	
District of Columbia	55		700	
Florida	112		774	
Georgia	87		755	
Maryland	67		363	
North Carolina	68		1,282	
South Carolina	32		179	
Virginia	66		419	
West Virginia	14		41	
West North-Central	333	7.6	3,238	5.1
Iowa	32		151	
Kansas	40		184	
Minnesota	125		1,872	
Missouri	103		842	
Nebraska	27		172	
North Dakota	5		14	
South Dakota	1		3	

Table 32 (continued)

Region and States	Foundations		Assets	
	Number	Percent	Amount	Percent
New England	357	8.1	2,298	3.6
Connecticut	108		811	
Maine	8		15	
Massachusetts	196		1,135	
New Hampshire	16		58	
Rhode Island	24		243	
Vermont	5		36	
Mountain	129	2.9	1,032	1.6
Arizona	24		233	
Colorado	54		550	
Idaho	6		20	
Montana	6		25	
Nevada	6		59	
New Mexico	8		49	
Utah	17		68	
Wyoming	8		29	
East South-Central	96	2.2	770	1.2
Alabama	24		107	
Kentucky	23		203	
Mississippi	10		33	
Tennessee	39		427	
Puerto Rico	1	—	1,108	—
Total	4,402	100.0	$63,075	100.0

Source: The Foundation Center (1985)

to the Foundation Center (1985), "remained fairly constant" from 1980 to 1984 and represented approximately 15 percent of total foundation awards. Social science grants gradually increased, rising from 5.7 percent of all foundation awards in 1980 to 7.6 percent in 1984. Grants to science rose slightly from 1980 to 1984 and represented 7.5 percent of foundation awards in the latter year. Grants to religion decreased in 1981 and 1982, but increased to 2.3 percent of all foundation awards in 1984.

As shown on Table 34, educational institutions are the primary recipient of foundation grants, receiving 35.1 percent of all awards in 1984. Although the 1984 share increased slightly over 1983, the portion is "still under the levels reported in the early 1980s" (The Foundation Center 1985). Moreover, although grants to public col-

Table 33

Foundation Funding Trends, 1980 through 1984 (Millions)

Category	1980 Amount	1980 Percent	1981 Amount	1981 Percent	1982 Amount	1982 Percent
Cultural	$ 161	13.5	$ 193	15.3	$ 209	14.0
Education	266	22.4	266	21.1	356	23.9
Health	299	25.1	283	22.5	312	20.9
Religion	29	2.4	25	2.0	28	1.9
Science	75	6.4	87	6.9	96	6.5
Social Science	68	5.7	75	6.0	102	6.9
Welfare	292	24.5	329	26.2	387	25.9
Total	$1,190	100.0	$1,258	100.0	$1,490	100.0

Category	1983 Amount	1983 Percent	1984 Amount	1984 Percent	1980 to 1984 Amount	1980 to 1984 Percent
Cultural	$ 277	15.4	$ 229	14.0	$1,069	14.5
Education	286	16.0	286	17.4	1,460	19.8
Health	390	21.7	390	23.7	1,674	22.7
Religion	38	2.1	38	2.3	158	2.1
Science	161	9.0	123	7.5	542	7.4
Social Science	132	7.4	126	7.6	503	6.8
Welfare	509	28.4	454	27.5	1,971	26.7
Total	$1,793	100.0	$1,646	100.0	$7,377	100.0

Source: The Foundation Center (1985)

leges and universities increased slightly, awards to private higher education institutions showed the "largest decline in the percentage of dollars reported" (The Foundation Center 1985).

The Establishment of Foundations

Nearly three-fourths of the 4,402 foundations in the *Foundation Directory* (1985) were established after 1950. As shown on Table 35, 3,168, or nearly 72 percent of the *Directory* foundations, were established after 1950, while 1,128, or 25.6 percent, were founded before 1950. The founding dates of 106 foundations, or 2.4 percent of the grantmakers in the 1985 sourcebook, could not be identified by the Foundation Center. The Foundation Center (1985) cites three main causes of the increase in foundations in the 1950s: 1) the emergence of company-sponsored and family foundations; 2) the "very high" tax rates then in effect; and 3) the "enormous societal needs" in the wake of World War II. However, the establishment of new

Table 34

Foundation Grants to Educational Institutions, 1982 through 1984 (Millions)

Institution Type	1982		1983		1984	
	Amount	Percent	Amount	Percent	Amount	Percent
Private Colleges and Universities	$345	54.4	$323	53.1	$279	48.3
Public Colleges and Universities	127	20.0	107	17.6	139	24.1
Graduate Schools	85	13.4	120	19.7	106	18.3
Elementary and Secondary Schools	73	11.5	53	8.7	47	8.1
Junior and Community Colleges	4	0.7	5	0.9	7	1.2
All Educational Institutions	$634	100.0	$608	100.0	$578	100.0

Source: The Foundation Center (1985)

Table 35

Decade of Establishment of Foundations in the 1985 *Foundation Directory:* Pre–1900 to 1984

Decade	Foundations Established	
	Number	Percent of Total
Pre–1900	38	0.9
1900–1909	20	0.5
1910–1919	68	1.5
1920–1929	141	3.2
1930–1939	183	4.2
1940–1949	678	15.4
Pre–1950	1,128	25.6
1950–1959	1,510	34.3
1960–1969	973	22.1
1970–1979	516	11.7
1980–1984	169	3.8
Post–1950	3,168	71.9
Data not available	106	2.4
Total	4,402	100.0

Source: The Foundation Center (1985)

foundations since 1950 has slowed, a phenomenon which the Foundation Center believes may be related to the increased regulation of foundations. The decline in new foundations notwithstanding, the Foundation Center (1985) contends that a "reasonable" growth period may develop because foundations have now had the "benefit of substantial (regulatory) experience."

The Regulation of Foundations

The Tax Reform Act of 1969 placed important restrictions on foundations and subjected them to taxation for the first time in American history. Although the 1969 law was amended in 1976 and in later legislation, the original regulatory emphasis remains in effect. Foundations pay a 2 percent excise tax on net investment income, a tax set at 4 percent in 1969 and reduced to 1 percent in 1985 for certain foundations. Also, most foundations are subject to an annual grantmaking requirement of 5 percent of the market value of assets. Other regulations restrict foundation activity in four areas: 1) political campaigns; 2) ownership of business; 3) administrative expenditures; and 4) "dealings between foundations and those who establish or manage them." Lastly, federal law requires foundations to file an annual report on assets and grants with the Internal Revenue Service and to make the report available for public inspection for at least 180 days. (See note.)

Summary: The Quantitative Dimension

The 4,402 foundations in the *Foundation Directory* (1985) represent 19 percent of the nation's estimated 23,000 foundations, but

For a detailed review of Congressional investigations and legislation affecting foundations, see *Patman and Foundations: Review and Assessment* (Andrews 1968); *Philanthropic Foundations* (Andrews 1956); "Some General Principles and Guidelines for Grant-Making Foundations" (Council on Foundations 1973b); *The Handbook on Private Foundations* (Freeman 1981); "Philanthropy and Politics: The 1983 Hearings" (Joseph 1983b); "Twenty-five Years and Change" (McCarthy 1984); *Trustees and the Future of Foundations* (Nason 1977); *The Big Foundations* (Nielsen 1972); *The Golden Donors* (Nielsen 1985); *Philanthropy in an Age of Transition* (Pifer 1984a); *Speaking Out* (Pifer 1984b); *Foundations Under Fire* (Reeves, ed. 1970); *U.S. Philanthropic Foundations* (Weaver 1967); and *The Philanthropoids* (Whitaker 1974).

held 97 percent of all foundation assets and made 85 percent of all foundation grants in 1983, the base year of the 1985 sourcebook. Assets of the 4,402 *Directory* foundations totalled over $63 billion, while their grants were over $4 billion. Independent foundations are the most prominent foundations in number, assets, and grants. Seventy-nine percent of the foundations in the 1985 *Directory* are independent foundations, and their assets represent 84 percent of all foundation holdings. The grants of independent foundations represent 71 percent of all foundation awards. The assets of *Directory* foundations have doubled since 1972, with the largest increase, 32.7 percent, occurring from 1981 to 1983. Grants of the *Directory* foundations have risen 163 percent since 1972. Nearly half the *Directory* foundations are located in eight northern states, but the South, Southwest, and Pacific regions are experiencing increases in the number of foundations.

From 1980 to 1984, welfare received over one-fourth of all foundation grants, while health, the second leading recipient, garnered nearly 23 percent. Education's share of foundation support declined from 22 percent in 1980 to 17 percent in 1984. Cultural activities, religion, science, and social science received approximately the same shares of foundation grants in both 1980 and 1984. Educational institutions are the leading recipients of foundation funds, but the share of foundation grants to such institutions decreased from 1980 to 1984. Moreover, private higher education institutions showed the largest decline in the percentage of grants awarded.

Nearly three-fourths of the *Directory* foundations were established after 1950, but over the last several decades, the number of new foundations has decreased, a phenomenon which the Foundation Center believes may be related to the increased regulation of foundations. Since the Tax Reform Act of 1969, as amended, foundations pay an excise tax on net investment income and must annually distribute 5 percent of the market value of assets. Foundations are prohibited from supporting political campaigns, while other regulations restrict their ownership of business, their administrative expenditures, and dealings with their founders or managers. Foundations must also submit an annual report on assets and grants to the Internal Revenue Service and make the report available to the public for 180 days.

Although the quantitative dimension provides an introduction to the number, type, assets, grants, and funding patterns of foundations, the orientation to foundations continues by examining their accessibility to grantseekers, the federal government, and the general public.

THE ACCESSIBILITY DIMENSION

"The overwhelming majority of American foundations ... have had, and continue to maintain, an obsession for privacy. ... Their preference to live in a cocoon is neither casual nor accidental. Most of them like that kind of existence ... and will attempt in so far as possible to preserve it."

Waldemar Nielsen
The Big Foundations (1972)

The Issue of Accessibility

The accessibility of foundations has been an issue since ancient Greece where foundations were highly suspect for political and economic reasons (James 1973). In the Roman era, Cicero believed that foundations had participated in the Catiline conspiracy, and during the Middle Ages, resentment of the Church's wealth from bequests was in evidence (James 1973). In the 18th and 19th centuries, critics in England charged that endowments inequitably controlled a large part of the country's wealth and that foundations were secretly influenced by *mortmain*, "the dead hand of the donor" (James 1973).

In the United States, accessibility was a major issue in the 1950s when Congress accused foundations of "interlock—a conspiracy to collaborate in order to subvert" (Joseph 1986a). In the late 1960s, during hearings for the Tax Reform Act of 1969, many of the criticisms against foundations concerned the secrecy of their operations (Freeman 1981). The Tax Reform Act of 1969, however, placed statutory reporting requirements on foundations, directing every foundation to make its Internal Revenue Service return available to the public for at least 180 days after filing. The annual return, called Form 990-PF, includes questions on income, expenses, assets, grants, and liabilities, as well as whether funds were used to influence legislation or participate in political campaigns. The reporting requirements enacted in 1969 reflect concern that "not enough information was available on what foundations do with their money" (Freeman 1981).

Individual Advocates of Accessibility

Long before the Tax Reform Act of 1969, leading foundation spokesmen advocated greater accessibility by foundations. Keppel, President of the Carnegie Corporation from 1923 to 1941, wrote that the fundamental safeguard against abuses by foundations is public opinion and the possibility of public controls (Magat 1984). Keppel believed that foundations should "operate with glass pockets" and that they could gain respect only through "complete disclosure of their activities" (Goulden 1971). He added that secrecy by one foundation damages the reputation of all foundations, and he often quoted Saint Paul: " . . . whether one member suffer, all the members suffer with it; or one member be honored, all the members rejoice with it."

Andrews (1956) believes that society cannot intelligently approve foundations unless it first understands them. Public reporting demonstrates public responsibility, he writes, and if foundations do not issue regular reports, "absence of reporting will itself become a significant danger signal."

> The public is entitled to know the facts—all the facts—about the operation of foundations. . . . They have a proud record (which) should be made accessible to public scrutiny. In no lesser way can the essentially public nature of the responsibilities of foundations be adequately demonstrated (Andrews 1956).

Simon, President of the Olin Foundation, believes that accessibility is in the practical interest of foundations. "They have to know what people are doing out there. Otherwise they can't do their job well" (Williams 1983). Buckman, President of the Foundation Center, indicates that because foundations are "elitist organizations" in a democracy, their need to be accountable is an "especially sensitive matter" (Williams 1984). Concludes Pifer (1984b): "I have always felt (that because) they are such privileged institutions . . . foundations should be judged by a higher standard."

Association Advocates of Accessibility

Leading philanthropic associations have also long encouraged full disclosure by foundations. The Council on Foundations (1973b), in its first policy statement on grantmaking, held that "out of the public trust vested in foundations grows the need (for) full disclosure (of) information about objectives and activities." In 1977, the National Committee for Responsive Philanthropy urged foundations to improve their accessibility, concluding that access must be widened to many organizations "presently shut out of the system." In its second policy statement, the Council on Foundations (1980) encouraged foundations to communicate with grantseekers through annual reports, newsletters, and other publications.

Joseph, President of the Council on Foundations, believes that accountability is now particularly relevant to foundations. Reporting on Congressional hearings on foundations, Joseph (1983c) urges that "unless we engage in self-regulation, we invite increased government regulation. No public presentation by the Council will be as effective as the private practices of foundations." In its most recent policy statement, the Council on Foundations (1984a) indicates that accountability extends "beyond the narrow requirements of the law," explaining that

> open communication with the public and with grantseekers . . . is in the interest of all concerned and is important if the grantmaking process is to function well, and if trust in the responsibility and accountability of grantmakers is to be maintained. . . .

The Inaccessibility of Foundations

The inaccessibility of foundations has been an issue for at least 50 years. Lindeman (1936) discovered 202 foundations on which he could acquire no information, while Hollis (1938) spent eight years of persistent inquiry to disclose mere basic facts on foundations. Hollis reported that the officers of foundations "did not wish to have those instruments investigated," noting that some officers considered his inquiry to be an "indiscretion," while others, although polite, were "just as firm in refusing information." Embree, who surveyed 505 foundations in 1949, was unable to get "any information at all" from 240 (Macdonald 1956), while Rich (1962) reports the "interesting and enlightening" experience of analyzing the Internal Revenue Service returns of more than 6,000 foundations between 1951 and 1955.

> In the course of this study, I was confronted by incomplete returns, several hundred letters from foundation trustees resentful of the availability of information about their activities, and occasionally cessation of filing returns. The high proportion of returns which were inadequately filled out prompted me, in 1953, to report my findings to the (Internal Revenue Service).

Chapper (1967) found that the Internal Revenue Service rejected one-third of foundation returns because of omissions, while in 1969, Andrews discovered that fewer than 60 percent of the returns were acceptably complete (Whitaker 1974). The Treasury Department's *Report on Private Foundations* (1965) concluded that many foundations

> continue in existence year after year without achieving any of the external indicia of unique advancement of philanthropy. They attract no public attention . . . gain no public support . . . open no new areas, develop no new vistas (and) create no rearrangements or alterations of focus among charitable enterprises generally.

In 1971, Magat surveyed New York City foundations to monitor their compliance with the Tax Reform Act of 1969, which requires foundations to place in a newspaper with "general circulation" a notice that their IRS form is available for public inspection. Magat found that 981 foundations placed their notice in *The New York Law Journal,* while 202 placed theirs in *The New York Times,* despite a circulation difference of 8,969 for the *Journal* versus 846,132 for the *Times.* Observed Magat: "However estimable *The New York Law Journal* may be in other respects, its circulation of 8,969 is somewhat less even than the 33,000 lawyers who practice in New York City" (James 1973). In 1974, the Grantsmanship Center wrote to the 5,454 foundations in the *Foundation Directory* (1971), stating that the letter was not a grant proposal, but only a request for publications for the Center's library. The Center received only 759 responses (14.5 percent) of which 532 (10.3 percent) provided useful information (Nason 1977). In 1983, Bothwell testified before Congress that 30 percent of the nation's 208 largest foundations refused to provide information about their activities after as many as six requests (Magat 1983b). In the same year, the General Accounting Office found that of 19 public information questions on Form 990-PF, nearly every foundation omitted at least one answer, and 70 percent omitted at least one-fourth of the answers (Gorman 1983a).

Crossland and Trachtenberg (1982) believe that grantseekers are justified in complaining about the information foundations make available. "Beyond question, most of us on the foundation side of the table do not do a satisfactory job of reporting accurately and in a timely fashion our policies and procedures." May, however, former Director of the San Francisco Foundation, describes the view on accessibility held by some foundations. "Well, look, if we're not breaking the law, we're all right, and don't tell me what else we ought to be doing, because you've got long hair and ideals" (Kennedy 1977). Concludes Pifer (1984a): "Various excuses for not (communicating) have been advanced by foundations ... but none of them are convincing. The record has improved slightly with time but is still reprehensible."

The Secrecy of Foundations

Despite legal requirements and the encouragement of individuals and associations, many foundations operate in secrecy. The "symptoms of this disease," explains Russell (1971), include

> offices with many doors—all closed; overprotective secretaries who won't let anyone in ... intercepted phone calls (and) little or no information about what the foundation is doing ... until the foundation is completely insulated from the outside world.

Table 36

Studies of the Public Disclosure Practices of Foundations, 1936 to 1983

Investigator	Year of Study	Findings
Lindeman	1936	Found 202 foundations on which no information could be secured
Hollis	1938	Spent eight years of persistent inquiry to disclose the most basic data on foundations
Embree	1949	Surveyed 505 foundations and received no information at all from 240 (reported in Macdonald 1956)
Rich	1962	Examined the Internal Revenue Service returns of 6,000 foundations, finding many incomplete returns and letters of complaint from several hundred foundations. Rich considered the number of improperly completed returns to be so high that she reported her findings to the Internal Revenue Service
Clapper	1967	Found that the Internal Revenue Service rejected one-third of foundation returns because of errors and omissions
Andrews	1969	Found that fewer than 60 percent of foundations' Internal Revenue Service returns were complete
Magat	1971	Found that 981 New York City foundations placed their required public notice in *The New York Law Journal*, while 202 New York City foundations placed their notice in *The New York Times* despite a circulation for the *Journal* of 8,969 versus 846,132 for the *Times*
Grantsmanship Center	1974	Surveyed 5,454 foundations in the *Foundation Directory* (1971), receiving only 759 replies (14.5 percent) of which 532 (10.3 percent) provided useful information (reported by Nason 1977)
Bothwell	1983	Testified that 30 percent of the nation's 208 largest foundations refused to provide any information after as many as six requests
GAO	1983	Reported that of 19 public information questions on Form 990-PF, nearly every foundation omitted at least one answer and 70 percent omitted at least 25 percent of the answers

Dickinson (1973) indicates that too many foundations do not communicate with consumers, their own communities, or anyone else.

> Some have shrouded (themselves) in a veil of secrecy; still others have never clearly defined their objectives; many have never published annual reports; still others have classified such reports top secret. Some foundations refuse to talk to a . . . grant applicant, even to tell him that his project is not of interest. Many do not acknowledge receipt of correspondence, let alone answer questions. . . .

The secrecy of foundations may reveal an "enclave mentality" which is central to the character of the institution (Nielsen 1972). Consequently, the public is sometimes irrational in its attack on foundations because people have traditionally lacked information on which to base thoughtful criticism (James 1973). In 1970, the Commission on Foundations and Private Philanthropy observed that by remaining a kind of closed society,

> foundations excited public suspicion that they were engaged . . . in secret things done in a dark corner. By their reluctance to discuss publicly their failures as well as their successes, the foundations . . . became instead symbols of secret wealth which mysteriously used the levers of power to promote obscure, devious, or even sinister purposes.

Foundations are "institutions like no others," concludes Nielsen (1985), operating in abstraction from external pressures and controls, according to their own "largely self-imposed rules."

> They are private, and yet their activities cut across a broad spectrum of public concerns and public issues. They are the only important power centers in American life not controlled by market forces, electoral constituencies, bodies of members, or even formally established canons of conduct. . . . (Nielsen 1985)

Reasons for Reticence

Coffman (1932) was one of the first researchers to discover the reluctance of foundations to share information, learning that many foundations believed that they were private organizations and had no responsibility to the public. Lindeman (1936) found the same reticence: "On the whole, (foundation) administrators continue to insist that wealth is a private possession and that the possessor may dispose of it as he pleases." Rockefeller (1973) explains that foundations often consider themselves "strictly private institutions" immune from public accountability, but a foundation's constituents are grantseekers, and they deserve an opportunity for dialogue—"a privilege they do not generally enjoy. . . . "

Joseph (1983e) indicates that foundations may shun publicity because of the tradition of anonymity in philanthropy. "Many people who engage in acts of private compassion do not seek public attention." Although a reluctance to boast about one's good works may be becoming modesty, at least one foundation, the Pew Memorial Trust, has claimed Biblical authority for doing its charity in secret (Nason 1977). The Russell Sage Foundation (1953) identified trustees of a large Chicago trust who believed that publicity was a "vulgar appeal for recognition. . . . " Moreover, while some foundations may consider publicity to be "undesirable self-advertisement," many more fear "the application a report may provoke" (Magat 1984). "Too many foundations still shun public information activity in the fear that it would bring a flood of new requests," adds Richman (1975). Writes Nason (1977): "More public information invites more requests for grants, and since there is never enough (money) to go around, this results in more disappointed people." Nielsen, however, believes that a deeper objection is that if foundations subject their programs to inquiry in the intellectual community, they would be forced into a humiliating debate because they "could not hold their own" (1972).

Despite concerns for modesty or the fear of more requests, Bothwell (1983) asks, "Without openness . . . how are charities and other non-profits that are unknown to foundation trustees and staff to have a serious chance of being considered for support?" Indeed, Freeman (1981) believes that publicizing foundation guidelines yields "fewer out-of-program requests." Clear statements of what a foundation does *not* do are as important as descriptions of its priorities (Freeman 1981). Adds Gottlieb (1986):

> A well conceived public relations program can produce an array of benefits for a non-profit organization or foundation: increased exposure among key donor groups, public awareness of . . . services and publications, wide dissemination of important research findings, and opportunities for collaboration and replication, to name a few.

Accordingly, asks Fenton, "What's the use of making a grant or creating a program if you devote little time to marketing it and no one finds out about it?" (Gottlieb 1986).

Disclosure in the Foundation Directory

The Russell Sage Foundation published the first directory of foundations in 1915, a sourcebook called *American Foundations* with only 10 pages and twenty-seven foundations (The Foundation Center 1985). Between 1915 and 1955, fourteen directories were published by the Russell Sage Foundation, the Twentieth Century Fund, Raymond Rich Associates, and the American Foundations Information Service. In 1955, Rich published a sourcebook containing "five times the number of foundations ever listed before," a feat which Magat (1984) attributes to Rich's "four-year labor (and) travel to no less than 60 Internal Revenue district offices. . . . " In the late 1950s, when the Foundation Center surveyed foundations for the first *Foundation Directory* (1960), it encountered "stiff opposition from a great many foundations," a response which James (1973) considers "difficult to describe as anything but reprehensible." The Foundation Center (1964) adds that many foundations threatened to sue if even public information was published. To test the validity of such complaints, the Center invented a foundation and gave it a small endowment and an address at the home of a staff member. The Center listed the "foundation" in the *Directory* with the notation: "Not in a position to entertain appeals of any sort." The Center reported: "No flood of mail materialized. In twelve months the 'foundation' received only ten letters from applicants and twenty-one pieces of junk mail" (Goulden 1971). The Foundation Center's current policy is to publish available information on all foundations, "whether or not they like the idea" (Williams 1984). "A small minority definitely does not like it," adds Williams (1984), "and even today the Center receives a few irate letters." Such responses notwithstanding, the Foundation Center notes that in 1984 and 1985, a record number of foundations responded to its questionnaire for inclusion in the *Directory* and that more foundations are now providing information to the public.

Publishing Annual Reports

Foundations have long been encouraged to publish annual reports, but only a small minority issue such summaries. Voluntary public reporting by foundations may have begun in 1867 with the Peabody Education Fund, "the first American foundation in the modern sense of that term" (Andrews 1956). When the Peabody Education Fund was established, its trustees declared, "A great Trust of this sort should have a permanent and public record. . . . Reports and Proceedings shall be stereotyped (sic) so that a complete series shall never be wanting in the Public Libraries of the Country" (1875). The trustees' attitude on reporting is further explained in the introduction to Volume I of the minutes.

> The Proceedings of the Trustees have been printed from year to year, and have been more or less widely circulated throughout the country. (However) the number of copies printed was insufficient for the demand which has since risen. . . . With this view, the present volume

Table 37

Number of Foundations in the *Foundation Directory* and its Predecessors, 1915 to 1985

Year	Publisher	Directory	Foundations in Directory
1915	Russell Sage Foundation	*American Foundations*	27
1948	Raymond Rich Associates	*American Foundations*	899
1955	American Foundations Information Service	*American Foundations*	4,162

According to Read (1986), fourteen directories of foundations were published between 1915 and 1955. Publishers applied varying criteria to select foundations, and the Foundation Center (1985) cites the 1915, 1948, and 1955 sourcebooks as representative of the first fourteen directories.

Year	Publisher	Directory	Foundations in Directory
1960	Foundation Center	*Foundation Directory*	5,202
1964	Foundation Center	*Foundation Directory*	6,007
1967	Foundation Center	*Foundation Directory*	6,803
1971	Foundation Center	*Foundation Directory*	5,454
1975	Foundation Center	*Foundation Directory*	2,533

Read (1986) reports that in the 1960 to 1975 editions of the *Foundation Directory*, less stringent inclusion criteria were used than are now applied. In 1960, for example, inclusion criteria were $50,000 in assets and $10,000 in annual grants. In 1975, criteria were $1 million in assets and $500,000 in yearly grants. From the 1977 to the 1985 editions of the *Foundation Directory*, inclusion criteria were $1 million in assets and $100,000 in annual grants.

Year	Publisher	Directory	Foundations in Directory
1977	Foundation Center	*Foundation Directory*	2,818
1979	Foundation Center	*Foundation Directory*	3,138
1981	Foundation Center	*Foundation Directory*	3,363
1983	Foundation Center	*Foundation Directory*	4,063
1985	Foundation Center	*Foundation Directory*	4,402

Source: Read (1986) and the *Foundation Directory*, selected years

> has been stereotyped and . . . all the succeeding Reports and Proceedings shall be stereotyped to conform to it. . . . (1875)

The John F. Slater Fund, established in 1882, followed the Peabody example. Wrote Slater (1882) in his letter of gift: "I desire that the doings of the corporation each year be printed and sent to each of the State Libraries in the United States, and to the Library of Congress." Annual reports began with the first year after founding for the Carnegie Institution of Washington, the Carnegie Foundation for the Advancement of Teaching, and the Carnegie Endowment for International Peace. The General Education Board began reporting in 1914, while the Carnegie Corporation, founded in 1911, issued its first report in 1921. Adds Magat (1984):

> Full disclosure was a policy of the Rockefeller Foundation when it was established in 1913, and its 1914 annual report—complete with financial transactions and holdings, descriptions of work performed by grant recipients, and photographs—would be a model even today. The Russell Sage Foundation, established in . . . 1907 . . . has published books and pamphlets since the beginning. . . . The Pew Memorial Trust took more than 30 years to publish its first annual report, but when it did, in 1979, it was pleased with the results. 'It was our hope,' wrote the (Pew) president, 'that such a report would attract the requests (to) improve the effectiveness of our work. The response has been gratifying' (Magat 1984).

Despite these examples, the record of foundations publishing annual reports is poor. Hollis (1938) discovered that approximately two-thirds of foundations did not publish an annual report and that many of the reports were "so general and condensed that they (were) for the most part meaningless. . . . " By 1956, seventy-seven foundations were issuing annual or biennial reports, and in 1966, this figure had increased to 127 (Nason 1977). In 1971, Goulden found that only 140 of the 30,242 foundations in the records of the Internal Revenue Service issued annual or biennial reports. Adds Goulden (1971): "Only seven of the ten largest foundations publish(ed) such reports (and only about) one-third of the 261 foundations with assets over $10,000,000 publish(ed) reports. . . . " In 1973, only 193 foundations, about 3 percent of foundations in the 1971 *Foundation Directory,* published annual reports (Friedman 1973). "Out of the 26,000 major American foundations, well over two-thirds have never published an annual report. The absentees include 79 of the 141 largest foundations" (Friedman 1973). In 1972, the Council on Foundations located reports by 246 foundations, by 307 in 1973, by 344 in 1974, and by 381 in 1975. Adds Richman (1975):

> Most of the 381 annual reports of U.S. foundations . . . are published by non-giants, although it is true that the larger the foundation, the greater the likelihood of it issuing an annual report. . . . It would be unrealistic to expect the smallest foundations—those distributing less than $25,000 a year—to publish reports. . . . This leaves the $25,000 a year or more class as the potential publishers (and there are slightly more than 6,000 foundations to which this applies).

Table 38

**Studies on the Number of Foundations Publishing Annual Reports,
1932 to 1985**

Author	Year of Study	Number Publishing Reports
Coffman	1932	73 percent of 75 foundations from 1921 through 1930 did not issue regular reports
Hollis	1938	two-thirds of foundations did not publish reports
Nason	1977	77 in 1956
Nason	1977	127 in 1966
Goulden	1971	140
Council on Foundations	1972	246
Council on Foundations	1973	307
Council on Foundations	1974	344
Council on Foundations	1975	381
Crossland and Trachtenberg	1982	465
Foundation Center	1985	625

Of the 100 largest foundations in 1975, 36 did not issue public reports, and of Richman's 6,000 foundations which might publish reports, only 7 percent did in 1977 (Nason 1977). In 1982, only about 465 of the approximately 26,000 foundations in the United States published annual reports, and even fewer reported their grants to the Foundation Center (Crossland and Trachtenberg 1982). In 1985, 625 foundations, or 14 percent of the foundations in the *Foundation Directory* (1985), published annual reports, although 30 percent of foundations in the sourcebook issued other public information materials (The Foundation Center 1985).

Many foundations that "fly below the radar screen" are small trusts administered by bankers, lawyers, or members of the donor's family (Crossland and Trachtenberg 1982). However, small foundations are not the only trusts which fail to publish reports, for twelve of the thirty-two foundations with assets over $100 million did not publish reports in 1971 (Friedman 1973). "More than half of total foundation assets are not represented in the annual report tally," concludes Friedman (1973), and "some of the richest foundations are among the worst-run and do not even reply to applicants" (Whitaker 1974). The failure of foundations to publish annual reports may be justified because the documents are expensive and may increase the number of grant requests, "many of which may only waste the time of both the asker and the asked" (Weaver 1967). However, whatever the rationale, none can outweigh the principle that foundations must account to the public for the stewardship of the public trust (Young and Moore 1969).

In recent years, foundations have become more accessible. "Communications is now a major concern in the foundation community," reports Magat (1984). But for every foundation that has made progress in communications, others are "still recalcitrant or mystified" about the process. After fifty years of failing to communicate with the public, foundations now face the choice of increasing their accessibility or continuing to be criticized by Congress, philanthropic associations, and the grantseeking community.

Summary: The Accessibility. Dimension

The accessibility of foundations has been an issue for at least half a century. Congressional investigations in the 1950s and 1960s disclosed the inaccessibility of foundations, leading to legislation encouraging foundations to increase accessibility. However, despite the recommendations of Congress, the Council on Foundations, the Foundation Center, and respected individuals in the foundation community, many foundations continue to strongly resist public disclosure of their activities. Participation in the *Foundation Directory* is low and the record of foundations publishing annual reports is poor. Therefore, although more foundations are implementing public information programs, the accessibility of foundations is still unacceptably and indefensibly low.

THE PERSONNEL DIMENSION

"Above all aspects of foundation work, I would put the human factor."

> Alan Pifer
> *Philanthropy in an Age of*
> *Transition* (1984a)

The Scarcity of Foundation Staff

Perhaps the most striking characteristic of foundation staff is their scarcity. Of the approximately 23,000 foundations in the

United States, only about 1,500, or 6.5 percent, employ full or part-time staff. Some 6,000 persons are employed by foundations, but only approximately half hold professional posts. Moreover, about two-thirds of all foundation staff are employed by only 400 foundations.

In 1970, the Commission on Foundations and Private Philanthropy found that 84 percent of foundations had no professional staff and that only 5 percent had full-time administrators. The Commission also learned that 58 percent of foundations with assets from $10 million to $100 million did not maintain full-time staffs. In 1972, Zurcher and Dustan reported that only 212 foundations employed 1,012 full-time administrators, of whom 83 percent were men and 17 percent were women. The authors identified 133 other foundations with 349 part-time employees, for a total of 345 foundations employing full or part-time staff. Commenting that foundations had "hardly reached the Stone Age" in employing staff, Zurcher and Dustan (1972) note that the

> acceptance of the concept of administrative staffing is still so tentative that the total number of individuals who derive their livelihood . . . from full-time employment in any foundation post above the clerical level is considerably less than the number of foundations.

Conclude Zurcher and Dustan (1972): "How minuscule these numbers are becomes apparent when they are compared with the estimated total of foundations. If the . . . figure of 24,000 is used as the estimated total, the staffed foundations do not exceed 1.5 percent of all foundations."

In 1984, the Council on Foundations learned that 417 foundations employed 3,916 full and part-time staff, about two-thirds of the estimated 6,000 persons in foundations (Boris 1984). Odendahl, Boris, and Daniels (1985) report that the number of staffed foundations has remained at approximately 1,500 and that foundations with over $100 million in assets employ over half of the full-time professionals.

The distribution of staff among foundations is quite uneven. Zurcher and Dustan (1972) found that approximately 25 percent of full-time administrators were employed by the Ford Foundation, while 15 percent served the Rockefeller Foundation, the second largest employer. Twelve percent were employed by eleven other funds including the Carnegie Corporation and the Commonwealth, Danforth, Duke, Houston, Kellogg, Kettering, R. K. Mellon, Mott, Rockefeller Brothers, and Sloan foundations. Thus, conclude the authors (1972), "thirteen major foundations employ about half of all full-time (foundation) personnel . . . in the United States."

The Recruitment of Foundation Staff

The recruitment of foundation staff, according to Weaver (1967), is a "little like picking candidates for a first trip to the moon." Although many characteristics are desirable, one cannot advertise for people with degrees of "bachelor, master, or doctor of philanthropy." Nason (1977) believes that skilled administrators are no easier to find for foundation work than for any other job. "Indeed," he writes, "the task may be harder. There are as yet too few to constitute a profession. There is no professional association (and) there is no professional training program" (1977).

A relationship with the donor is a key factor in the employment of many foundation administrators. Andrews (1956) explains that if there is a "common denominator" among foundation staff, "it is association with the donor." Adds Nielsen (1972):

> (Foundation) employment is the result of a personal association with the donor or an influential trustee rather than educational or professional qualification. In earlier times the foundation officer tended to be a former 'private secretary' of the donor. More recently he seems to be a lawyer who has served the donor or his company, a junior executive of the company, or a retired educator. . . .

The entry of foundation staff to philanthropy is marked by an "element of adventitiousness," for if a person were to consider a career in philanthropy, he would be "hard put to know where to start" (Zurcher and Dustan 1972). Of 298 staff members surveyed by Zurcher and Dustan, only ten said that they had planned or prepared for foundation service. Andrews (1956) reports that few foundation executives consciously sought their jobs. Rather, recruitment is often a combination of "acquaintanceship, fitness, and accident, in varying proportions." Access to foundation positions is quite limited, and although more posts have recently been created, the foundation community is still small and interconnected (Odendahl, Boris, and Daniels 1985). Report the authors (1985):

> Almost all of the foundation employees we interviewed obtained their positions because they were familiar with the field, had a contact at a foundation, or knew someone who did. Age, gender, and type of education contribute to the formation of personal and professional networks (which influence the recruitment of foundation staff).

Foundation executives confirmed the importance of networks in securing employment. Said one: "I had a friend who had his ear very close to the ground. He called me up." Said the director of a company-sponsored foundation: "I used my contacts in the company to get this job. I had a lot of contacts." Another foundation

Table 39

Recruitment Methods of a Sample of 49 Foundation Executives

Recruitment Method	Foundation Executives	
	Number	Percent
Recruited	30	61.2
Letter or Personal Visit (a)	8	16.3
Network Contacts	7	14.3
Advertisement or Employment Agency	4	8.2
Total	49	100.0

(a) from a foundation officer or trustee

officer said that one of his graduate school professors, who was a consultant to a foundation, may have helped him. "I'm not sure what role he played in my getting the job. I think I might have had him down as a reference." Another officer said that his foundation, which was looking for a "young lawyer," called professors at Harvard, Yale, and Columbia and asked for recommendations. The director of a family foundation said that he obtained his post in a "typically capricious way."

> A board member of this foundation kept asking me to do it. This is quite common in foundations dominated by family. They're looking for people likely to be comfortable with them. And it's not likely to be someone that they didn't know before. Professional talent is too far removed from that personal tie. Nobody came out of a competitive job search in this area. There is no one who did not have some personal connection, no matter how tenuous (Odendahl, Boris, and Daniels 1985).

Because personal contacts appear to be key in obtaining foundation employment, vacancies are rarely advertised. Odendahl, Boris, and Daniels (1985) found that of a sample of 49 foundation executives, only four, or 8 percent, were employed through an advertisement or employment agency. On the other hand, thirty executives, or 61 percent, were recruited by foundations, while "personal visit," "letter," and "network contacts" accounted for the employment of fifteen executives, or over 30 percent of the sample. Thus, as shown on Table 39, nearly 92 percent of the sample of foundation executives said that they had been recruited for their posts through personal contacts. One foundation officer explains that through the " 'old boy network,' " candidates are "tapped (and) need not apply. They may not even deign to apply." Explains another foundation director:

I knew the foundation because I knew the former executive director. He was a friend of mine. . . . I've known a member of the board for a long time. He is also a member of the board of the (organization where I had worked). I guess he suggested my name as a possible candidate (Odendahl, Boris, and Daniels 1985).

The Professions of Foundation Staff

Foundation staff come from a variety of professional backgrounds including higher education, government, law, research, and business. The directors of 40 large foundations studied by Andrews (1956) came from business and finance, academe, law, social work, publishing, medicine, and engineering. However, such categories may conceal an even greater variety of experience, for the director of one foundation "was himself an engineer, attorney, economist, fundraiser, and author" (Andrews 1956). Among the prior positions of foundation officers interviewed by Goulden (1971) were:

a vice president of a drug company; a professional engineer . . . a Wall Street attorney; a law professor; a public relations director for a small manufacturing concern; an assistant director of the Job Corps . . . a vice president of labor relations of an oil company; a professional fundraiser . . . an advertising man; and a president of a small college.

Zurcher and Dustan (1972) found that 61 percent of the prior positions of foundation staff were in higher education, other non-profit organizations, and the federal government. Of fourteen occupational areas, however, the most popular as a stepping stone to foundation employment is college and university teaching or administration. Table 40 shows the concentration of prior positions in higher education, non-profit organizations, and government. Ten years after Zurcher and Dustan found that only 4 percent of foundation staff had served in other foundations, Boris (1982b) discovered that the portion had risen to 30 percent. However, noted Boris (1982b), "Some of this movement undoubtedly reflects growth while some reflects staff turnover." The increase in foundation staff notwithstanding, Boris (1982b) reports that 29 percent of the executive directors said they were the first executive employed by their foundation. After the category of employment in other foundations, education was the second leading previous employer, providing posts for 22 percent of foundation staff. Business, with 21 percent, was the third leading prior occupation. Employment in a community organization ranked fourth with 11 percent, and government, with 7 percent, and law, with 5 percent, were the other leading previous occupations of foundation staff (Boris 1982b). Weaver (1967) contends that most foundation officers are from academe, "simply be-

Table 40

Prior Occupational Areas of Foundation Staff

Occupational Area	Percent of Foundation Staff
Higher Education	37.0
Non-Profit Organizations	12.1
United States Government	12.1
Corporate Manufacturing or Marketing	8.7
Communications	6.8
Banking, Investment, and Insurance	4.9
International Agencies	4.5
Other Foundations	4.2
Self-Employed Business or Profession	3.4
Other (state and local government, secondary school teaching or administration, fine arts, armed services, and miscellaneous)	6.3
Total	100.0

Source: Zurcher and Dustan (1972)

cause there is such a wide overlap of education and philanthropy." Explains Weaver (1967): "Academic presidents have left to become foundation officials; foundation officials have resigned to become academic deans and presidents." Branch (1971) agrees: "University teaching and administration emits (sic) the largest number of philanthropic professionals for the foundations. . . . " Odendahl, Boris, and Daniels (1985) found that although not all foundations executives had worked in academe, the proportion is high enough to support that stereotype. One foundation officer explained the similarities between the academy and foundations:

> I think that (the relationship) is very understandable, and that it has been going on for a long time. I think the jobs are really quite comparable. . . . The administrative skills are very comparable (and) of all the jobs I could think about, the job that comes closest (to being a foundation officer) is academic work (Odendahl, Boris, and Daniels 1985).

Branch (1971) notes that foundation officers come not only from higher education, but also from the Pentagon and defense industry. Whitaker (1974) adds that the connection between foundations and the federal government is "remarkable." He explains that

> *Henry Kissinger* . . . used to be Director of the special studies project at the Rockefeller Brothers Fund. *Dean Rusk* . . . was President of the Rockefeller Foundation (and) a special Rockefeller fellow. . . . *John*

Gardner ... was President of the Carnegie Corporation of New York. ... The former Secretary of State, *J. F. Dulles,* had been chairman of the Carnegie Endowment trustees; and *Dwight Eisenhower* had also been a trustee. *Robert McNamara* ... (was) a trustee of the Ford Foundation and of the Robert Kennedy Memorial Foundation. ... *Douglas Dillon* ... Secretary of the Treasury ... (served) as chairman of the Rockefeller Foundation. Ford's President, *McGeorge Bundy,* (was) a special assistant for national security (in the Kennedy administration). ... (Kennedy's advisor *Arthur Schlesinger, Jr.* (was) a trustee of the Twentieth Century Fund ... *John McCloy* (of the Central Intelligence Agency) was a trustee of the Rockefeller Foundation. ... *Eugene Rostow* ... was a trustee of the Meyer Research Institute. ... *Nelson Rockefeller* was assistant Secretary of State for Latin America. ... *George McGovern* (was) a trustee of the Danforth Foundation (and) *Cyrus Vance* (and) *Bill Moyers* (were) both Rockefeller trustees. ...

Whitaker (1974) found that in 1961, the Council on Foreign Relations included ten of fifteen Ford trustees; twelve of sixteen Sloan trustees; ten of fourteen trustees of the Carnegie Corporation; twelve of the twenty Rockefeller trustees; and thirteen of the twenty trustees of the Twentieth Century Fund. Macdonald (1956) reports that many Ford Foundation staff members were connected with the government or one of the "committees, commissions, councils, agencies, associations, societies, institutes, boards and bureaus without which Americans seem unable to do anything. ... " Former jobs of Ford Foundation staff, according to Macdonald (1956), included Program Director for the International Trade Organization, Chief of the Division of International Security Affairs of the United States Department of State, President of the Alaska Rural Rehabilitation Corporation, Director and Research Director of the Chicago Council on Foreign Relations, Research Director at the Applied Social Research Bureau at Columbia University, and Field Director of the Division of Program Surveys in the United States Bureau of Agricultural Economics.

Nielsen (1972) believes that people enter philanthropy for several reasons. The salaries, compared with those in government and the university, are "good; the perquisites are excellent; and job security is unexcelled." Adds Nielsen (1972):

There is range and diversity in the problems one deals with and in the contacts one makes; and there is the feeling that one is 'doing good.' The field has a particular attraction for the well-educated, the idealistic, and perhaps the insecure.

"For the academic," explains Nielsen (1972), foundation work is a way to "get out of the ivory tower and into contact with more con-

Table 41

Highest Educational Degrees of Foundation Administrators

| | Foundation Administrators | |
Highest Degree	Number	Percent
Doctorate	96	34.5
Bachelor's	66	23.7
Master of Arts	46	16.5
Law	33	11.9
Medicine, Master of Business or Public Administration	23	8.4
None	14	5.0
Total	278	100.0

Note: Data are from personnel in "managerially advanced" foundations. In less "managerially advanced" foundations, the findings are consistent, except that the doctorate is held by fewer foundation administrators (18.1 percent in less "managerially advanced" foundations versus 34.5 percent in "managerially advanced" foundations.

Source: Zurcher and Dustan 1972

crete problems." For the government official, foundation service can be an escape from the burdens of bureaucracy or an uncongenial administration. Nielsen (1972), however, believes that why foundation staff enter the profession is "something of a mystery," for foundation officers are subject to much disparagement by grantseekers. Explains Nielsen (1972):

> The general public may regard philanthropic work as relatively prestigious, but in the academic and scientific community foundation officers are often considered second-rate individuals whose credentials would not qualify them for the faculties and staffs of first-rate universities or research centers. Similarly, many figures in intellectual life tend to think of them as bureaucratic functionaries. Although many government officials view foundation employment at times with some envy, they also think of it as a refuge for people who have retired to the periphery of affairs.

The Education of Foundation Staff

Many foundation staff members have advanced degrees. Of 278 foundation administrators studied by Zurcher and Dustan (1972), only fourteen (5.0 percent) did not hold at least a bachelor's degree. As shown on Table 41, the doctorate was the highest degree of the largest number of staff (34.5 percent), while the bachelor's degree was the highest of the second largest number of staff, nearly one-fourth of the sample. The master of arts degree was the highest of

16.5 percent of the sample. A law degree was the highest of 12 percent of the sample, while degrees in medicine and master's degrees in business and public administration were the highest degrees of 8 percent of the sample.

The abundance of doctorates among foundation staff is confirmed by Goulden (1971), who reports that nineteen of twenty members of the Rockefeller Foundation's agricultural sciences division are Ph.D.'s, as are eleven of fourteen persons in the division of humanities and social sciences. Wortman, director of the Foundation's agricultural sciences division, explains that "we look for people who want to sign aboard Rockefeller for life, and the PhD tells us that they are good" (Goulden 1971). The Foundation's own policy statement seems to suggest the importance of advanced degrees.

> The very nature of the foundation's programs requires a high level of professional quality and sustained effort toward defined goals. In order to achieve progress on an international scale, work must be supported over long periods of time. . . . Such programs require the long-term services of qualified professional staff dedicated to the foundation (Rockefeller Foundation 1968).

Boris (1982b) found that 62 percent of foundation staff had advanced degrees—32 percent with doctorates or law degrees and 30 percent with master's degrees. Over half had their highest degree in either the humanities (28 percent) or social sciences (23 percent). Business is next (14 percent), followed by law (10 percent), education (8 percent), and math and sciences (6 percent), according to Boris (1982b).

Many foundation staff members graduated from private colleges and universities. Odendahl, Boris, and Daniels (1985) report that over half of the staff members they sampled were graduates of private institutions, and approximately 20 percent graduated from "Ivy League universities." In the New York City foundations, 75 percent of foundation staff were educated at private schools, but in California, foundation officers are more likely to have received their degrees from state colleges and universities (Odendahl, Boris, and Daniels 1985).

Women and Minorities in Foundations

In 1972, Zurcher and Dustan described the influence of women and minorities in foundations in one sentence: "With token exceptions, the world of the staffed foundation is still a white world and a man's world, and this fact does not appear to cause too serious concern among those who govern and manage foundations." (See note.)

Since the 1970s, the number of women in foundations has increased, but men still dominate, especially at the senior level. In 1981, although six out of ten foundation staff members were female, only one of five chief executive officers was female (Boris and Unkle 1981). Explain the authors:

> Women hold most of the administrative assistant and support positions. At the professional level, it is only in program officer and mid-level positions—including office managers, accountants, assistant treasurers—that women fill about half the jobs (1981).

Boris and Hooper (1982) report that women who do manage foundations tend to work in small foundations, and Boris (1982b) adds that women now account for over one-fourth of the chief executive officers. In 1983, Odendahl and Boris (1983a) reported that women held 43 percent of the executive and professional staff positions at foundations, although Boris (1984) adds that more than half of the women are directors of foundations with less than $10 million in assets.

Among the prominent examples of women in executive posts in foundations are Margaret Mahoney, head of the Commonwealth Fund; Anna Faith Jones, head of the Boston Foundation; Terry Saario, head of the Northwest Area Foundation; Elizabeth McCormack, principal advisor to the Rockefeller family; and Susan Berresford, Vice President of the Ford Foundation (Nielsen 1985). Although Viscusi (1985b) believes that for women, philanthropy is

Whitaker (1974) identifies ten characteristics of foundation trustees. They are mainly mature, white, wealthy, conservative, Protestant males from business, law, or finance who are graduates of eastern private colleges and universities and have a personal or professional relationship with the donor or the family of the donor of the foundation. The final trait of trustees is their pluralism. Whitaker (1974) learned that many trustees serve on multiple foundation boards. Nason (1977) estimates that there are 110,000 foundation trustees in the United States, or slightly more than four for each of the nation's 25,000 foundations. Foundation boards are becoming more diverse. The Council on Foundations reports that women comprise 25 percent of foundation trustees and minorities represent 5 percent. There are now more trustees under 40 years of age and fewer over 70. The United States Congress, the Council on Foundations, the National Committee for Responsive Philanthropy, and individual members of the foundation community are encouraging greater diversity on foundation boards.

"now a field in which opportunities seem plentiful," Nielsen (1985) contends that "on the whole," philanthropy is still comprised of "male-dominated institutions (especially in) senior executive and professional staff positions."

Minorities represent a smaller portion of foundation personnel than do women. In 1972, Nielsen discussed the scarcity of minorities in foundations, noting that although the "WASP homogeneity" is being diluted by a small but growing number of blacks, the appointments are mostly at the specialist, not the chief executive level. Contending that many foundations are "glaring examples of institutional racism," Nielsen (1972) states that in the employment of minorities, foundations are far behind the federal, state, and local government; churches; and universities. Writes Nielsen (1972):

> It is an ironic commentary on institutions that have long contended that education is the avenue by which blacks could move to a place of equality in the American system that they themselves have been generally unwilling to admit blacks to their own ranks—even though well-qualified blacks have been available for at least forty years, often as the result of foundation assistance.

In 1982, Boris reported that minorities comprised 13 percent of all foundation staff, 10 percent of professional posts, and 17 percent of support positions. Only 1 percent of chief executive officers, however, were minorities. In 1985, having witnessed an increase in the number of minorities in foundations, Nielsen reported that blacks held four of the top posts in the field: James Joseph, President of the Council on Foundations; Franklin Thomas, President of the Ford Foundation; Clifton Wharton, Chairman of the board of trustees of the Rockefeller Foundation; and Steven Minter, Director of the Cleveland Foundation, the oldest of the community foundations.

The number of women and minorities in foundations has increased in recent years, but generally remains below their representation in other organizations. Although women historically occupied the lower-level positions in foundations, they now hold approximately one-fourth of the chief executive officer posts, predominantly, however, in smaller foundations. Minorities comprise 13 percent of all foundation staff, but only 1 percent of chief executive officer positions, despite their leadership of such influential philanthropic organizations as the Council on Foundations, the Rockefeller Foundation, and the Ford Foundation.

The Salaries of Foundation Staff

Salaries of foundation staff vary by the size and type of foundation. In large independent and operating foundations, salaries are

Table 42

Median Annual Salaries of Foundation Staff, by Position and
Type of Foundation

| | Type of Foundation | | | |
Position	Independent	Company	Operating	Community
Chief Executive Officer	$56,300	na	$56,300	$40,000
Program Officer	40,000	40,000	40,000	33,000
Office Manager	$25,600	$25,600	$25,600	$20,500

Source: Boris 1984

generally higher than those in other foundations (Boris 1984). Zurcher and Dustan (1972) found that salaries of foundation staff are not as high as those of corporation executives, but are consistent with those in government and higher education. The authors compared the salaries of foundation program officers with the weighted average salaries of full professors in 1969–70, finding that full professors in private universities earned $23,299, a figure in the "middle range" of the salaries of program officers (Zurcher and Dustan 1972; American Association of University Professors 1970). According to Zurcher and Dustan (1972), salaries of program officers ranged from $16,000 to $35,000, with most in the area of $25,000.

In 1984, Boris studied the salaries of foundation chief executive officers, program officers, and office managers in the four types of foundations. As shown on Table 42, chief executive officers of independent and operating foundations had the largest annual salaries, with a median of $56,300. The salaries of chief executives of community foundations averaged $40,000. Among program officers in independent, company-sponsored, and operating foundations, the median salary was $40,000, while program officers in community foundations earned a median annual salary of $33,000. Office managers in independent, company-sponsored, and operating foundations earned a median annual salary of $25,600, while their counterparts in community foundations earned $20,500.

Recommended Attributes of Foundation Staff

Although foundation staff bring a variety of skills to their employment, certain qualities are recommended by authorities. Andrews (1956) looks for people who have a "great deal of common sense (and) absolute integrity and imagination." Foundations want variety in the training of staff, he adds, but the important element is that they are responsible, honest, imaginative, and are willing to work very hard. With the latter requirement, Weaver (1967) agrees: "I myself have worked harder and longer, and with far less vacation time, for foundations than I previously did for a major technical institute and a major state university."

Nason (1977) believes that foundation staff need "administrative competence and professional knowledge combined with imagination, integrity and humility. . . . " Freeman (1981) contends that although administrative experience is valuable, more important are integrity, intellectual curiosity and imagination. "Writing ability (is a) useful tool, but the ability to listen and sensitivity to the aspirations of others are essential." Moreover, if a foundation's money is to be spent well, foundation officers must be able to exercise judgment and make decisions (Freeman 1981).

Pifer (1984a) contends that the attitude and behavior of foundation staff are most important.

> If they are arrogant, self-important, dogmatic, conscious of power and status, or filled with a sense of their own omniscience—traits which the stewardship of money tends to bring out in some people— the foundation they serve cannot be a good one (Pifer 1984a).

"If, on the other hand, they have genuine humility, are conscious of their own limitations, are aware that money does not confer wisdom, are humane, intellectually alive and curious . . . the foundation they serve will probably be a good one" (Pifer 1984a).

Interesting yourself in other people's goals is essential, writes Weaver (1965), and there are people who "cannot do it." There are also people who can—who find publicly unobservable satisfaction in knowing that they have helped. "A good philanthropoid," writes Weaver (1965), "must be one of this latter breed." However, the consideration of recommended attributes for foundation staff may be somewhat fruitless, for the job is a "little like a parachute jump. . . . You close your eyes, swallow hard, and 'hit the silk.' Having survived one test, you proceed to the next—and the next—and the next" (Weaver 1965). Macdonald (1956) reports that the typical Ford Foundation "philanthropoid," a term coined by Keppel, first President of the Carnegie Corporation, is "serious, even idealistic, about his work and gives every evidence of enjoying it." When he has lunch—"at Schrafft's (in New York City)—with other foundation staff, he is used to such kidding as, 'Have you spent your million for today yet?' " (Macdonald 1956)

The one attribute for foundation staff, however, rated above all others, is "soundness of judgment, (a) tenuous quality," partly innate but able to be developed through education and experience. For foundation service, the tradition of the "able and adaptable amateur—the generalist"—still has considerable value. Although there may be no consensus on the skills required for the work, the most important qualification for philanthropy, in the words of one foundation officer, is "common sense" (Odendahl, Boris, and Daniels 1985).

Summary: The Personnel Dimension

Among the personal, educational, and professional characteristics of foundation staff, perhaps the most striking is their scarcity, for only about 1,500 of the nation's 23,000 foundations employ staff. Some 6,000 persons work in foundations, but only approximately half hold professional posts, and two-thirds of all foundation staff are employed by 400 foundations. A relationship with the donor is a key factor in the employment of many foundation administrators, and the professional entry to philanthropy has an "element of adventitiousness" (Zurcher and Dustan 1972), for few administrators admit to having planned for foundation service. Vacancies in foundations are rarely advertised, but rather, are often filled through the personal contacts of foundation donors or trustees. Foundation staff come from a variety of professions; most notably, government, service organizations, and especially higher education. Although not every foundation administrator worked in academe, Odendahl, Boris, and Daniels (1985) believe that the proportion is "high enough to support that stereotype." A 1972 study by Zurcher and Dustan found that only 4 percent of foundation executives had worked in another foundation. Ten years later, Boris discovered that the portion had risen to 30 percent, suggesting an influx of staff to foundations.

Many foundation staff members have advanced degrees. A study of 278 foundation administrators by Zurcher and Dustan (1972) showed that only fourteen, or 5 percent, did not hold at least a bachelor's degree. In 1982, Boris found that 62 percent of foundation administrators had advanced degrees—32 percent with doctorates or law degrees and 30 percent with master's degrees. A study by Odendahl, Boris, and Daniels (1985) showed that over half of foundation executives were graduates of Ivy League colleges and universities.

Women, who historically occupied lower-level posts in foundations, now hold about a fourth of chief executive officer positions, predominantly, however, in small foundations. Minorities represent 13 percent of foundation staff, but only 1 percent of chief executive officer posts, despite their leadership of influential philanthropic organizations including the Council on Foundations, the Rockefeller Foundation, and the Ford Foundation. Annual salaries of foundation administrators in 1984 ranged from a median of $56,300 for the chief executives of independent and operating foundations to $20,500 for the office managers of community foundations. Chief executives, program officers, and office managers in independent, company-sponsored, and operating foundations generally earned more than their counterparts in community foundations.

Authorities recommend that foundation officers possess several qualities including integrity and imagination, administrative competence, writing and speaking ability, diligence, curiosity, and humility. However, the attribute which was rated above all others in a 1972 study by Zurcher and Dustan was "soundness of judgment," a tenuous quality, but one which is essential to the central function of foundations, grantmaking.

V

THE PROCESS AND DIFFICULTY OF GRANTMAKING

"A really good grant represents a conjunction of the stars. . . . It is a rather large order and one that is not likely to be filled to everyone's complete satisfaction this side of the millennium."

Frederick P. Keppel
The Foundation: Its Place in
American Life (1930)

Purpose of the Chapter

This chapter examines the process of grantmaking, focusing on its subjectivity and difficulty, as well as the efforts of foundations to articulate grantmaking criteria. The tasks of foundation officers are described, as are the dangers of isolation and arrogance which can accompany the distribution of charitable funds.

THE GRANTMAKING PROCESS

The Act of Grantmaking

Grantmaking is the act of selecting institutions to receive funds. Grantmaking is not a scientific process, but rather, is based on the assumption that judicious funding decisions are possible. Although grant decisions are seldom arbitrary, they are neither totally objective, for organizational and individual values are always present. Thus, there is "no precise measuring stick" to select a potentially successful project (Odendahl and Boris 1983b).

Friedman (1973) believes that grantmaking is unstructured, and that criteria on grant decisions are "subject to many variations." Grantmaking criteria are often not explicit, write Odendahl and Boris (1983b), and the grantmaking process is "rarely described" and "too rarely discussed." Much of the process is "either secret or at least not public," reports Friedman (1973), a phenomenon making the analysis of grantmaking as difficult perhaps as the process itself.

Grantmaking Criteria

Although grantmaking can be subjective, foundations have attempted to develop criteria to guide the process. In the early days of the Rockefeller Foundation, an imaginative trustee is reported to have said, "Our policy should be to have no policy" (Weaver 1967). This intention notwithstanding, Fosdick (1952) reports that after the first meeting of the Rockefeller Foundation, a "Memorandum on Principles" was adopted with six grantmaking criteria:

> 1. Individual charity and relief (are) not to be considered. 2. Projects of a purely local nature (are) to be excluded, unless they (are) in the nature of a demonstration. 3. No permanent good could be anticipated by giving aid for any purpose that (is) incapable of provoking a desire on the part of the recipient to assist and carry it forward. 4. Outside agencies should not become permanent or indefinite charges. 5. Gifts in perpetuity to other institutions should not have tight restrictions. 6. Preventive projects (are) to be preferred over projects of a palliative type.

"What are the criteria of a 'good grant?' " asks Goodwin (1976). "Hard to say." Landau (1975) found only one book on foundation grantmaking (*The Management of American Foundations*, Zurcher 1972), but contends that its treatment of the topic is "brief and incomplete." Despite these observations, Weaver (1967) believes that foundations need a "well-defined and clearly-announced program" to make competent judgments. The Council on Foundations (1980 and 1984a) agrees:

> Whatever the nature of the entity engaged in private grantmaking, and whatever its interests, it should seek to establish a set of basic policies that define the program interests and fundamental objectives

to be served. . . . The processes for . . . deciding on grant applications should be established on a clear and logical basis . . . consistent with the organization's policies and purposes.

Goodwin (1976) contends that financial criteria are useful in evaluating grant requests, and he proposes several questions to evaluate grantseekers:

Has the grant applicant depended on a few major contributors, or has funding come from a broad constituency . . . indicative of wide interest . . . in the organization's programs? What have been the applicant's major areas of expenditure and what relative percentages have been directed to program or administrative areas? Are the applicant's financial personnel knowledgeable and capable? What has been the experience of other grantors with the applicant?

Weaver (1967) believes that foundations cannot afford to consider the value of one project without seeing the attraction of others, for foundations are obliged to think more broadly and more objectively about grant requests. "How many are there? Do they . . . represent a total field of activity that the foundation . . . should get into? Is there any reason . . . strategic, social, intellectual, or moral . . . for preferring (one opportunity over another)?"

According to the Council on Foundations (1984b), grantmakers have developed several "operating principles" to guide their decisions. The first and foremost of these policies, explains Joseph (1986e), is itself the *"concern with principles;"*

the idea that the practices of foundations should reflect (and) reaffirm values (for) the word (principles) gives us a powerful symbol with which to grasp . . . what is fundamental when we decide on priorities, choose among grantseekers, commit resources and otherwise serve a public good. . . .

Although grantmaking principles "are (only) beginning to emerge," Joseph (1983e) believes that they are important because "poorly focused . . . grantmaking programs serve no one well—neither the donor interested in maximum return nor the donee interested in maximum resources." As foundations have become more professional, explains Viscusi (1985b), greater concern about grantmaking principles has developed. The Council on Foundations (1984a) agrees, indicating that principles have two advantages. "They provide a framework for consistent, effective practice, and they afford the public a view of ethical and philosophical values on which grantmaking organizations base their conduct." Warm (1979) identifies two trends that have encouraged foundations to sharpen the focus of their grantmaking. First, there has been an "increasing commitment to (the) management of foundation(s) . . . and the grantmaking process." Second, the number of grant requests has "grown substantially," increasing the competition for funds. However, Warm (1979) reports that despite this impetus, "serious misconceptions continue to exist about the grantmaking process." One of the most frequent complaints of grantseekers, writes Macdonald (1956), is that they are "up against an intricate slot machine that might pay off or might not, according to its own arcane mechanical logic." A trustee provides an example of such logic in one foundation.

> Well, we don't know much about what we're doing, but we sure have a nice time doing it. Every December the chairman invites all of us to dinner. We have a few drinks and a good meal and a lot of laughs. After dinner he tells us how much money we have to give away, and we all pitch in with ideas on who to give it to. I usually suggest my college. Somebody else will tell about his niece who is working for a charity. I've always liked the girl, so we include the charity. And of course somebody's wife is always on the board of something or other, so we include that. It doesn't take much time (Goulden 1971).

Although this trustee may believe that foundation grantmaking is easy, the literature holds otherwise, for philosophers, philanthropists, and foundation officers have commented extensively on the difficulty of wise grantmaking.

THE DIFFICULTY OF GRANTMAKING

The Tasks of Foundation Officers

Macdonald (1956) explains that foundation officers screen "thousands of applications," investigate fields for funding, "think up problems worth solving," and select institutions or people to try to solve them. Andrews (1956) adds that foundation staff determine "what types of grants shall be made . . . to what agencies (and) under what conditions. . . . " Are controversial projects to be avoided or chosen? Should large or small grants be made, and should grants go to individuals, agencies, or colleges and universities? Through all these decisions, concludes Macdonald (1956), foundation officers "carry on the negotiations, often protracted, and the inquiries, often delicate," to determine that "this enterprise shall be nourished . . . while that one shall not."

"A Wearisome and Complicated Business"

Menninger (1981) writes that grantmaking is "wrought with complications," and Macdonald (1956) confesses that it is a "wearisome and complicated business, vexing to the soul and wearing on the liver." Aristotle was one the earliest observers of the difficulty of grantmaking, noting that to give money away

> is an easy matter and in any man's power . . . but to decide to whom to give it, and how large a sum, and when, and for what purpose, and how is neither in every man's power nor an easy matter. Hence, it is that such excellence is rare and praiseworthy and noble (Macdonald 1956).

Weaver (1965) reports that many of his friends thought his job was very easy, "for what it amounts to is getting rid of money and they have no trouble . . . getting rid of theirs."

> But giving away money *wisely* is quite another thing. It is an extraordinarily subtle and difficult task, with moral, social, and intellectual complications that keep your conscience alive and your mind bothered (Weaver 1965).

Stern (1966) agrees, noting that many people fault the Ford Foundation's approach to grantmaking. "But when I ask them how they would spend the quarter of a billion, the glibness fades." To give money away wisely involves patience, insight, courage, hard work, disappointment, regret, and worry. Adds Menninger (1981): "There are surprises, sometimes unpleasant ones; there are contests of values, swings of preference, paralyzing ambivalences, pet peeves and hobbyhorses."

If foundation officers experience the difficulty of grantmaking, so, too, have many philanthropists. John D. Rockefeller searched in vain for a scientific approach to grantmaking, instead of "haphazard methods of giving it away" (Kiger 1954). Marquis (1923) reports that Henry Ford was "besieged" by grant requests totaling as much as $6 million a month. Kellogg, according to his doctor, was deeply frustrated. "In my long practice of psychiatry, I don't know of a more lonely, isolated individual" (Nielsen 1985). Rosenwald, founder of the Sears, Roebuck Company and the Rosenwald Fund, said it was more difficult to grant a million dollars than to earn it (Young 1965), and Carnegie was frustrated with the "supremely difficult art of spending large sums of money" (Wall 1970). Carnegie himself said that he had not worked one-tenth as hard at making money as he had at giving it away. By 1906, he was so disheartened that he wrote, "You have no idea of the strain I've been under. Millionaires who laugh are very, very rare indeed" (Wall 1970).

The Subjectivity of Grantmaking

Grantmaking is an art, not a science, for despite grantmaking criteria, subjective judgments are necessary (Freeman 1981). Hollis

(1938) was an early observer of the subjectivity of grantmaking, indicating that the task is "neither an automatic or a routine clerical job."

> There can be no rule-of-thumb measuring of applications by unvarying and predetermined policies. The decision to make or refuse a grant is usually a complicated cultural understanding involving ... the intelligence, knowledge, ambition, bias, and idiosyncrasy of donors, trustees, operating staff, and advisors.

Keppel said he had to "play by ear and proceed by hunch" in grantmaking (James 1951), while Pifer (1984a) reports that the Carnegie Corporation taught him the "mysteries" of being a foundation officer. Mayer (1972) refers to the "strange world of giving money away," and Magat (1983a) believes that grantmaking can be "a rote process, a lottery, a congeries of guesswork, a charade of whim."

Macdonald (1956) notes that grantmaking is often "boring, unsatisfying, even irritating," reporting that foundation officers complain of a "curious sense of unreality." Hoffman, returning to private industry from the Ford Foundation, said he was happy to get back to the profit and loss statement. "Now I know just where I am every month. Never did at the Foundation" (Macdonald 1956). Another foundation officer reports that there is

> no way of telling whether (you are) using (the money) wisely or not, because there's no competition, no criticism. You won't get fired if you fail—and anyway no one could be sure that you *were* failing. No one ever got fired from a foundation for doing a bad job—only for sticking to a principle (Macdonald 1956).

Ruml, once head of the Rockefeller Memorial Fund, writes that grantmaking is very corrupting and "gives you a feeling of complete insecurity" (Macdonald 1956), while Nielsen (1972) concludes that foundation officers work in an "unreal landscape where the hot sun never blazes, the cold winds never blow, and failure does not exist."

The subjectivity of grantmaking causes some foundation staff to approach their task with detachment and to contend that the best grants are made "with the head, not the heart." Nonetheless, Pifer (1984b) believes that there is a place for the heart in foundation work. Carnegie, however, when criticized for not giving with his "heart as well as his head," replied, "The heart is the steam in the boiler; the head is the engine that regulates dangerous steam and prevents disastrous explosions" (Whitaker 1974). Pifer notes that in baptisms in the Episcopal Church,

> one prays that the child will become a person of 'discerning heart.' That ... is not a bad term for a sound approach to grantmaking (be-

cause) grantmaking with the head alone is fully as dangerous as grant-making only with the heart (1984b).

"A Genius for Charity"

During Congressional hearings in 1952, foundation officers cited a "scarcity of the gifted or talented for foundation work—who have that oft-mentioned 'feel' or 'touch' " as one of the field's major problems. Twenty-five years later, Nason observed a lack of "management ability" in foundations, reporting that in a nation which has elevated managerial skills to a high art, the "paucity of such skills in the philanthropic world is the more conspicuous." Thoreau (1854) wrote, "You must have a genius for charity as well as anything else," perhaps understanding the qualities required for foundation officers.

Keppel (1930) identifies some of the skills of the foundation executive.

> He must be immune to cajolery (and) must be . . . a good 'waiter.' He must (be) well-informed. . . . And he must accomplish and direct all this without so complicating his existence that he loses his power to see the forest rather than the trees.

Perkins (1965) contends that listening is the most difficult part of the job.

> It is particularly hard for a young man off an academic campus (whose) function (it was) to talk while it was the function of the students to listen. To get into an office where he is to spend minutes and hours listening and listening and listening is very important but very hard.

Lyman (1982) believes that foundation officers must have the capacity to derive vicarious satisfaction from the achievements of others. Adds Weaver (1965): Foundation officers need a "large streak of unselfishness. Interesting yourself in other people's goals and ambitions is essential. . . . " Magat (1983a) adds that judgment is the essential requirement of foundation staff, explaining that

> no robot can take the place of the program officer who turns proposals round and round in his or her professional lens. That lens combines technical training, experience on both sides of the grantmaking table, idealism or skepticism, faith or cynicism, intuition or reliance on the judgment of respected individuals (1983a).

Andrews (1956), however, believes that the job also requires unlimited curiosity, sympathy, and "extraordinary ability to get along with people" including the trustees who are the final authority, disgruntled grant applicants, lunatics and self-appointed world saviors, grantees who turn out prima donnas, (and) the pitiful who seek help.

"To Do More Harm Than Good"

Pritchett (1922) was an early observer of the potentially injurious effect of grantmaking: "Somebody must sweat blood with gift money if its effect is not to do more harm than good."

> All giving . . . cuts more than one way. Ofttimes the byproducts of giving, even of giving to a good cause, result in social toxins which do enough harm to more than counteract the benefit that may come from the original gift (Pritchett 1922).

Notes Ylvisaker: "I have often mused over the irony that we in philanthropy attempted to improve society by using the affluence which has in many ways softened and corrupted it" (Whitaker 1974). Adds Bundy: "How destructive it can be to make the uplifting of others the means of one's own self-esteem" (Whitaker 1974). "How easy it is to do harm in wishing to do good!" writes Turgot.

> To foresee with certainty that an establishment will produce only the effect desired from it. . . . To discern . . . the real evils which a long series of unseen causes may bring about—this would (require) the most profound genius (Stephens 1895).

Todd (1930) writes that man sometimes does nothing so badly as "his attempts to go good."

> If mortal man is endowed with a definite instinct to do good, that alone is . . . sufficient cause for doubting the value of mere instinct as a guide to civilized social life. . . . But if we reject instinct as a basis for doing good, have we not cut the ground from under our feet? For what alternative can we depend upon? Common sense? The advice of friends? All these are slender reeds. Can we turn to science, then, to guide us? Is there any science of doing good? (Todd 1930)

The Isolation of Grantmakers

Grantmaking can create a sense of severe isolation in foundation officers. Foote (1985) lists several "occupational hazards" of foundation staff including "professional isolation . . . smugness (and difficulty in) establishing relationships with grantees, board members (and) peers." Reports Foote (1985): "People get burned out giving money away. People in . . . foundations . . . feel isolated."

According to Brim (1973), the isolation of grantmakers is manifest in five ways. First, foundations officers operate with a high degree of autonomy. "No voters elect them and no stockholders judge their actions." Second, there is no objective way to evaluate them. "There are no performance statistics; no batting average; no earned-run average (and) no bottom line. . . . " Third, foundation executives are "socially encapsulated." Many foundation officers are "eastern, male Wasps . . . surrounded by friends and colleagues from the same background. . . . " Fourth, foundations "rarely deal in truth in exchanges with applicants." Explains Brim: "When one is appointed to a foundation post, the usual line is, 'Congratulations, you'll never have another bad lunch, or hear another honest word . . . ' " Fifth, foundations are not often criticized. "While there are some occasional critics . . . there is a virtual absence . . . of criticism compared with what is received by . . . universities, hospitals, government, and corporations" (Brim 1973).

The impersonality of foundation work troubles many grantmakers. The sense of isolation, of being "cut off from intellectual and scientific peers," troubles others (Nielsen 1972). Odendahl, Boris, and Daniels (1985) learned that foundation officers are cautious when associating with applicants. Said one staffer: "You are never really on a person-to-person basis, because always you are the funder, and they are always guarding themselves." Said another, shortly after obtaining his post: "I lost my last true friend (and) heard my last honest compliment" (Odendahl, Boris, and Daniels 1985). Reports a more experienced officer:

> I worked in a large foundation for almost 10 years and never heard an honest statement from anybody on the outside. . . . If you say something stupid at a cocktail party, people aren't going to say you're wrong. They'll bend with you. I've seen professors who have worked on a subject for years bring their proposal to a program officer who will usually make some inane suggestions. But the professor usually agrees, even if it means substantially shifting the focus of his work (Branch 1971).

Concludes Andrews (1956): "Criticism, however bitterly felt, is buried beneath a smiling surface so long as a grant, or another grant, is in prospect . . . In this as in other cases, no one shoots Santa Claus."

Despite isolation and impersonality, there are compensations in foundation work. "Hopeful applicants for grants keep luncheons from being lonely, and even modest stories are certain of uproarious reception" (Andrews 1956). One of the unexpected pleasures for a new foundation officer is being the center of discussion.

> He suddenly finds himself at the focus of attention at social and professional gatherings where persons of importance take him aside to talk to him about their current project. His words on almost any sub-

ject are listened to with unaccustomed respect; even his pauses are taken to be significant. He is touched, in short, by the aura of power which the vast wealth of the foundation creates (Nielsen 1972).

Foundation officers, however, may lead somewhat unreal lives. "The deference, the red carpet treatment, the unremitting emphasis on future possibilities . . . can produce a dangerous degree of self-satisfaction," explains Lyman (1982). Miller, when at the Ford Foundation, felt that everyone wanted something from him—"a feeling such as a rich man or a pretty girl (has). . . . You'd see someone advancing on you at a party, and you'd think, O.K., cut out the next twelve stages" (Whitaker 1974). Magat (1983a) considered many of the social invitations he received to be a "stroking technique" to lay the groundwork for proposals. At a cocktail party, the Gaithers of the Ford Foundation were introduced as the Gaitshills. "They had a fine time until the hostess discovered her error," reports Macdonald (1956), "after which everybody began to talk projects to them." Said Hutchins: "It's a nice job. You meet so many *interested* people" (Macdonald 1956).

Foundation staff are sometimes the targets of personal animosity from applicants, for although officers may receive "public flattery," they are often held in "private disrespect" (Nielsen 1972). Crawshaw and Bruce (1978) believe that an emotional exchange occurs between grantmakers and grantseekers, and that grantmaking can be "punishing" for foundations. The gift not yet repaid debases the man who accepted it, explains Mauss (1925), a phenomenon causing some grantees to verbally abuse foundations. Both grantseekers and foundations, therefore, are "not free of suffering" (Crawshaw and Bruce 1978).

Foundation officers are also frustrated because they are only superficially involved with the work of grantees. Foundation staff are "only workers in the vineyard," explains Macdonald (1956). "They don't plant the vines and they don't drink the wine." Although foundation staff may have some of the powers of the philanthropists, they are not themselves rich and powerful donors (Odendahl, Boris, and Daniels 1985). Therefore, they occupy an uneasy position between grantseekers and foundation trustees.

> Foundation workers have to be . . . aware of the changing style required for presentation of self as they are facing outward toward the public and potential grantees, and as they face inward in presentation of their views and wishes toward the board of directors. . . . (Odendahl, Boris, and Daniels 1985)

"In short," add the authors, "the paradox for the executive is that he or she may appear arrogant and intractable to applicants and yet have to appear humble and at least tractable to board members" (1985). Foundation officers are also insulated from exchange and evaluation.

> They are cut off from the natural flow of evaluative information that other institutions receive in American life. They do not know whether they are doing what they think they are doing—or whether what they are doing makes any difference to anyone or not (Brim 1973).

Because of the secrecy of philanthropy, adds Nielsen (1972), foundation staff are insulated from the criticism to which the scholar is normally exposed. Accordingly, such isolation may breed "narcissism and illusions of feelings of power," separating foundation administrators from the "frontiers of thought" (Brim 1973).

"Does efficiency (in grantmaking) breed emotional distance, separating gift, giver and recipient?" ask Crawshaw and Bruce (1978). Macdonald (1956) believes so. "(The foundation officer) does feel something impersonal, and therefore unreal, about his work."

> This impersonality has several unexpected results. One is a curious resentment it seems to create in people against an institution that operates entirely for their own good. . . . (Also, grantseekers resent foundations which) give money away out of vanity or even less admirable motives (or) on the basis of knowing what will be best for other people (Macdonald 1956).

"We don't want to play God," a Ford philanthropoid tried to explain. "We only want to diffuse creativity and thought" (Macdonald 1956). However, said another officer, "When I am trying to decide between applications from researchers in the same field . . . I can't help feeling like I play God. . . . "

> I know that what I decide is going to have a profound effect upon this man and his family, not only for the grant year but for the rest of his professional life. . . . What I am deciding, really, is whether this guy's wife has to take a job teaching at an elementary school . . . so that he can afford the year, or whether they'll get our money and have fairly normal lives (Goulden 1971).

"People here (claim that they are) 'strictly objective' in grantmaking (but) what I do here in one morning can make or break a man's career, the difference between (bringing) him a Nobel or leaving him in the corner as an assistant professor of humanities" (Goulden 1971).

The Danger of Arrogance

Arrogance is a common, if unattractive, characteristic of some foundation officers. "Succumbing to the seductions of the God complex," explains Menninger (1981), "is a real occupational hazard."

Staff members sometimes find it hard to remain properly humble when they believe they are brighter, and certainly wiser, than either the Board or the (grant) seekers. Having money to give away and the power to decide whom to give it to is intoxicating, and foundations can be irritating examples of the 'narcissism of the righteous' (Menninger 1981).

A foundation officer told Zurcher and Dustan (1972) that he relishes the power and prestige of the job: "No one can deny (that) such power is ego-building and, frankly, helpful in stimulating and encouraging others to move in a given direction. I like this power." Said another officer: "You begin to think it is your own money, the longer you are in foundation work. . . . You want more and more discretion. You want more and more authority. You begin to think you know everything about everything" (Odendahl, Boris, and Daniel 1985). Miller, head of the philanthropies of the Cummins Engine Company, explains that every job has its occupational virus. "Ours is . . . arrogance. . . . "

The ability to withhold or dispense is a heady feeling indeed. . . . We can say to the supplicant across the desk any outrageous thing, crack any terrible joke. He must nod sagely and laugh at the right places (1984).

Adds Miller: "The first consequence of arrogance is that we, who are in such great need of wisdom, so often do not hear any voice save our own. . . . Our own ideas and our own biases become enclosed in sanctuaries" (1984).

Laski (1930) reports that grantseekers may contribute to the arrogance of foundation staff. When a foundation officer visits a higher education institution, for example, he meets people who are "keenly alert to . . . his own interest" and eager to explain that this is the very thing they are "anxious to develop in (their) university" (Laski 1930).

When you see him at a college, it is nothing so much like the vision of an important customer in a department store. Deferential salesmen surround him on every hand, anticipating his every wish, alive to the importance of his good opinion, fearful lest he be dissatisfied and go to the rival across the way. The effect on him is to make him feel that he is shaping the future of the social sciences (Laski 1930).

"The longer I work in this field," concludes Somerville, "the more I feel we would all do well to take an advanced course in modesty" (1983).

"No Little Buoyancy of Spirit"

An occupational hazard of philanthropy, explains Pifer (1984a), is repeated exposure to the financial plight of others. "While the reaction may at times be a kind of relieved 'there but for the grace of God . . . ,' more often it is one of deep concern, even anxiety." Menninger (1981) believes that grantmaking places special burdens on people who are motivated by a desire to serve. The psychological costs of this objective often include

> chronic depression; a pervasive sense of doubt about one's effectiveness or sense of self-worth; obsessional worrying and behavior that sometimes makes decisions almost impossible; (and) an enormous need to be liked and to be seen as helpful by others (Menninger 1981).

James (1951) adds that foundation officers find that the world's woes have become an "oppressive obsession."

> Altruists who are melancholy, reformers who are mournful, 'low-spirited humanitarians,' saints who are spoil-sports instead of being 'happy warriors'—we have all known a few of them (James 1951).

"They prove," he concludes, "that a man who devotes himself to (this) sort of work had better be endowed with no little buoyancy of spirit."

Summary: The Process and Difficulty of Grantmaking

Despite claims by laymen that giving money away is easy, the literature holds that grantmaking is extraordinarily difficult. Philosophers, philanthropists, and foundation officers have commented on the difficulty of the task, noting that the job requires curiosity, empathy, and above all, uncommonly fine judgment. Foundation staff speak of the ambiguity, subjectivity, and impersonality of grantmaking, referring often to their loneliness and isolation. Moreover, grantmakers confess that they are not without arrogance and bitterness, particularly when they are targets for envy and animosity from grantseekers. Observers and officers of foundations, therefore, cite consistent evidence of the considerable difficulty of grantmaking.

VI

THE GRANTMAKING PRINCIPLES
OF FOUNDATIONS

"Grant makers, be they trustees or staff, rarely articulate the philosophical tenets that they apply in the practice of their art. (It) is not common for the foundation philanthropist to set down in writing for others to see the more philosophical principles or guidelines that he or she applies to grant making."

Patrick Kennedy
Preface to "Guidelines on Grantmaking" by Lindsley F. Kimball
Foundation News
March/April 1974

Purpose of the Chapter

This chapter proposes six principles which underlie the grantmaking decisions of foundations. The principles are: 1) foundations consider grantmaking as an investment; 2) competent grantseekers are necessary; 3) realistic proposals are important; 4) the clarity of many grant proposals is weak; 5) the continuity of grant programs is essential; and 6) a partnership between grantor and grantee is needed.

INVESTMENT: THE FIRST
GRANTMAKING PRINCIPLE

"I do not give alms; I am not poor enough for that."

Friedrich Nietzsche
Thus Spake Zarathustra

Grantmaking as an Investment

Grantmaking as an investment has received wide attention in the literature on foundations. The "very notion" of philanthropy, explains Pattillo (1973), implies "purposeful" giving, for grantmaking is more than "merely disposing of money;" the act must be guided by a "constructive purpose." The investment principle may derive from the prevailing attitude in foundations that "social stability is good" (Young 1965). Explains Cannon (1921):

> The philanthropists belong to a class on which the injustices of our present basis of society have not borne heavily. They serve unconsciously as the bulwark of the *status quo*, for whose defects they are ready and eager to apply palliatives. They are the great menders and patchers-up of society. . . .

Although many foundations portray themselves as energetic and innovative, they are mainly traditional and non-controversial. Their activity is "conventional, not reformist." They are institutions of "social continuity, not change." Their programs are "neither ideological nor activist," neither to the right nor to the left, but "down the middle of the road" (Nielsen 1985).

The 1952 House Select Committee reported that only 1 percent of foundations considered their grants to be risky, while the 1970 Commission on Foundations and Private Philanthropy estimated that only 3 percent of foundation grants were innovative. In 1972, Zurcher and Dustan reported that "more than 68 percent" of foundations considered their grants to be "supportive" and that most foundations were engaged in the "distinctly conventional subsidization of churches, universities, museums, and local charities. . . . "

Nielsen (1972) believes that foundations are similar to bankers, preferring applicants who are "familiar, who can present good credentials, and who are generally 'sound.' " Adds James (1973):

> Foundations generally have stayed . . . at the conservative-banker end of the grantmaking continuum . . . playing the solid, low-risk, socially and politically acceptable conservative game. . . . Little more than this

can be realistically anticipated. . . . The gnawing question for the future is whether that will be enough.

The conservatism of foundations differs significantly from the popular belief that they provide "venture capital." In fact, very few foundations award "risk money." Most of their funds are "invested in 'blue chip' " agencies and institutions very nearly as they would be spent "by those who made or inherited (them)" (Young 1965). John D. Rockefeller, who created his fortune by "meticulous attention to efficiency," thought the same methods should apply to philanthropy (Whitaker 1974). Explains Rockefeller (1908):

> Certainly one's ideal should be to use one's means, both in one's investments and in one's benefactions, for the advancement of civilization. . . . Our investments not less than our gifts have been directed to . . . multiply (and) diffuse as universally as possible the comforts of life. . . . These are the lines of largest and surest return.

Kimball (1974) relates an article in which Rockefeller wrote, "If anyone comes to me and says, 'Without your help this project will die,' I always say no because I don't want to play God (or) take the responsibility for life or death for any undertaking." The Rockefeller Foundation's original "Memorandum on Principles" appears to support the industrialist's belief, for one of its six points was, "Preventive projects (are) to be preferred over projects of a palliative type" (Kiger 1954). Like Rockefeller, Carnegie (1900) believed that "indiscriminate charity" is a serious obstacle to good philanthropy.

> It is better for mankind that the millions (of dollars) of the rich were thrown into the sea than so spent as to encourage the slothful, the drunken, the unworthy. Of every thousand dollars spent on charity today, it is probable that nine hundred and fifty dollars is unwisely spent—so spent, indeed, as to produce the very ends which it hoped to mitigate or cure. . . . (Carnegie 1900)

Kimball (1974) considers grantmaking as a purchase; "that is, you buy the steak and not the sizzle. You answer for yourself the question, 'What is left when the money is gone?' "

> I once turned down a request . . . to finance the American Legion parade up Fifth Avenue and was soundly berated by the national commander, who said, 'Can't your foundation ever do anything patriotic?' I said, 'Sure, I would think the discovery of penicillin could be called patriotic—a foundation fellow did that.' 'Oh,' said he, 'I know, but research isn't enough. Can't you ever take part in things closer to life?' 'Well,' I said, 'tell me what is left when the parade is over and I'll buy that. . . . '

"It is better to lick yellow fever," concludes Kimball (1974), "than to build hospitals to take care of the patients."

Grantmaking as Risk-Taking

Grantmaking as risk-taking has received wide support in the literature on foundations. Vincent believed that foundations must take risks, rather than supporting only "tested projects" (Dodge 1928). Half the foundations answering a survey by the 1952 House Select Committee said their "primary purpose" was providing venture capital (Kiger 1954). Henry Ford II testified that it is better make mistakes trying to solve problems than to leave them unsolved, while Hutchins said that foundations should go where other institutions "dare not or cannot go." Andrews (1956) believes that foundations have a "mandate" to take risks, for they are generally free from political controls. "Foundations have no external constituency, no voters, customers, or advertisers," adds James (1973). Therefore, "in theory at least," they can operate on the "cutting edge of innovation."

Many foundations, however, have a "fear of failure" which leads them away from untried ideas (Newton 1969). One test of a good foundation, he adds, is the number of grants it makes on "calculated long shots, some of which must fail." Foundations which do not take risks, according to Friedman (1973), may become irrelevant as social institutions. "To be above the battle is to be irrelevant," concurs Ross (1981); "to be irrelevant is to risk controversy." However, every grant may be inherently controversial because it involves the "taking of sides—in one of two ways."

> (The) recipient of even the blandest . . . foundation grant is likely to be an institution whose structures or policies are the subject of contention. For example, museums seem . . . safe enough—and yet more than one museum has been accused of paving over its parking land, representing too few black artists (or having) too few young people on its board. . . . (Simon 1973)

Although foundation philosophy supports risk-taking, few foundations take risks. The "vast majority" of foundations, according to Nielsen (1972), "avoid taking any risk," and even "activist" foundations venture forth "only hesitantly and infrequently." Innovation and risk-taking are often "latent or potential" qualities in foundations, rather than "existing attributes" (Friedman 1973). The Commission on Private Philanthropy and Public Needs (1975) concluded that many foundations are less willing to take risks than the government. Adds Young (1970): "Foundations avoid controversy like the plague," reflecting instead the "Matthew Syndrome" (Whitaker 1974): "For unto everyone that hath shall be given, and he shall have abundance; but from him that hath not shall be taken away even that he hath" (Matthew XXV, 29). Stern (1966) believes that the size of a foundation is a determinant of its level of risk-taking. "That which is large will never be crusading," he explains. McCloy, a Ford Foundation trustee, agrees: "It's hard to be daring in a big foundation. You're constantly being forced into conventional grooves by criticism or the fear of it" (Macdonald 1956). The theory of risk-taking, concludes Hechinger (1967), is noble, but the practice is "conservative, cautious, and distinctly noninnovational."

The lack of risk-taking by foundations may derive from the conservatism of their trustees. In their "eternal quest for dignity," many foundation trustees avoid being pioneers (Branch 1971). For a proposal to be approved by "half a dozen ... self-important critics," adds Embree, it has to be "almost so 'sound' as to be innocuous" (Whitaker 1974). "The new that we tried," reports Ylvisaker, was more often a "novelty to the donor" than a societal innovation. "The risks we took were still guaged in terms of the reactions we got from the members of our own club" (Whitaker 1974). Trustees dislike disturbing themes, concludes Laski (1930), and because people often give money to people they know, " 'dangerous' problems are not likely to be investigated."

Foundations may prefer making grants to safe institutions because they are easier to evaluate. Explains Dollard: "It takes more careful study, more careful investigation to make a grant of $5,000 to one individual than it does to give a grant of a half-million to a well-established university. . . . " (Macdonald 1956). Adds Nason (1977):

> It takes less time and thought to make a grant to the Metropolitan Museum of Art than to search out and support young and relatively unknown artists (as well as less trouble to) endow a new professorship than to fund an unorthodox approach to the problem of academic tenure.

"It is so much more work to listen and to try to hear," writes Miller (1984), to discover in a poorly written proposal the "treasure of an idea."

Despite the conservatism of foundations, Rockefeller (1973) asks, what chance will the "small man with the big thought" have in acquiring funding from the government? What corporation will make a risky grant? "Who but the foundations are left to explore the creative potential of unproven applicants?"

> Who else in the 1920s and 1930s would have provided funds to give advanced training to a generation of black leaders ... ? Who else would have financed the Myrdal study on the American racial dilemma in the 1940s ... ? Who else would have created a commission

on public broadcasting, financed the Conant study of the American high school, and created the Kerr Commission on higher education? (Nielsen 1972)

"Who else," asks Nielsen (1972), "would have put up the money for *Sesame Street?*"

These examples notwithstanding, foundations may be avoiding important issues at a time when imagination and risk-taking are needed. "Our horizons are too close," concludes Miller (1984); "our vision too dim. . . . " As the world becomes more confusing, foundations appear to be "impelled to play it safer and safer."

COMPETENCE: THE SECOND GRANTMAKING PRINCIPLE

"Money is enabling but only men produce."

Lindsley F. Kimball
"Guidelines on Grantmaking"
Foundation News
March/April 1974

"To Find the Good Men and Back Them"

If foundation grantmaking is an investment, foundations must carefully evaluate several key characteristics of grantseekers, the first of which is their competence. The "most ancient and useful" rule of foundations, explains Gardner, is to "find the good men and back them" (Whitaker 1974). A talented person can make an impressive performance even though the plan he submits is faulty, but the best plan will not ensure success if the man involved is incompetent (Whitaker 1974). The success of a grant request, therefore, often depends "less on the project" than on a foundation's estimate of the person advancing it (Macdonald 1956).

Carnegie believed that the essence of grantmaking is to "find the efficient man and enable him to do his work" (Hollis 1938), while Josephs (1945) explains that money is "not given for an idea," but rather, to a person with the "force and skill" to fulfill the idea. When evaluating grant proposals, Mayer (1972) asks,

What is the track record of the institution? Is it highly regarded in its specific field of interest? Does it have the human resources to carry out its proposal (and) will the project benefit from able, efficient, and reliable management . . . ?

"Are the persons involved dedicated and unselfish as well as experienced and competent?" adds Weaver (1967). "Do (their) past records . . . justify confidence?"

Of the criteria influencing grantmaking, Kimball (1974) believes that "first and foremost" are the persons involved. He explains that

> the best program the Rockefeller Foundation ever had was its fellowship program, because this developed the ablest persons who could be found around the world. . . . Every single fellow was hand-picked . . . and among the 10,000 fellowships awarded through the years there were not only . . . 30 Nobel laureates, but also leaders in every field of endeavor (Kimball 1974).

Townsend (1974) learned that 100 foundations and government grantors considered competence one of five "very much" to "absolutely important" factors in grant decisions. The other four important criteria are "purpose," "feasibility," "community need," and "applicant accountability." DeBakey (1977) judges research projects on the investigator's education and training, experience, competence, and promise, while Sibley (1951) believes that money alone is not an effective substitute for the human mind.

Johnson's fourth of five reasons to deny a grant request focuses on competence. In a fictitious letter rejecting a proposal, he writes, "There isn't any evidence in what you've said to us that you know much about what you're doing. . . . " (1975d). Magat (1983a) indicates that often an initially "drab project on paper" becomes exciting because of "unique staff resources." However, finding competent grantseekers is not easy because they are not always associated with institutions. "Are all geniuses professors?" asks Weaver (1967). "Are there not individuals of outstanding ability who do not fit into the disciplined and regimented systems of orthodox institutions?" The son of the founder of the MacArthur Foundation urged the foundation to award grants to "maverick geniuses," contending that Einstein could not have written a grant request saying that he planned to discover the theory of relativity (Nielsen 1985). Branch, however, believes that giving money to "unknowns" presents a double risk.

> First, unknowns are less predictable and therefore more prone to controversy. . . . (Second) unknowns are . . . more prone to failure—if only because they lack the credibility to *declare* their projects a success. . . . 'I see it every day,' said one Ford (Foundation) staff man. 'If a dean calls up from the University of Kansas, he is lucky to get listened to at all. (But if a dean from Harvard calls) you unconsciously respond more to the Harvard dean. I do it myself, even though I promise not to' (1971).

Much of grantmaking, writes Allen (1965), consists of "sizing up persons" and estimating their potential. Therefore, grantmaking may be considered as a "bet on an individual" (Freeman 1981). Rockefeller reports, however, that selecting individuals to receive funds can be dangerous.

> In the Rockefeller Family Fund . . . we place more emphasis on the quality of an individual than on the track record of an organization. This can be risky. When an individual is key to the quality of a project, that same individual's interest and participation generally determine the project's life span. Nevertheless, we believe that change is often the result of the personality and commitment of one person, and we are willing to take risks to identify such people (1973).

As a solution to the difficulty of selecting persons to receive grants, Weaver (1965) suggests that foundations ask, "Who are the 'better young people,' the up and coming people," reporting that certain names will emerge "over and over." Judging younger persons, however, is an especially challenging problem because of their generally short experience (Weaver 1967).

The notion that "money can create ideas" and that more money can create better ideas is a fallacy, writes Fosdick (1965), for without competent grantees, money will purchase nothing but "motion and futility." "Yet," notes Menninger (1981), "we persist in the fantasy that 'money makes the difference' (and that money) can make the problem go away." But all that money can do, concludes Andrews (1956), is provide time and tools to a person of "vision and ability."

REALISM: THE THIRD GRANTMAKING PRINCIPLE

> "Nothing is more illuminating in the study of (grantseekers) than to note the wide gap between the accomplishment which they consider themselves to have compassed and that which unprejudiced and impartial observers credit them."
>
> > Henry S. Pritchett
> > "A Science of Giving"
> > *Annual Report of the Carnegie Corporation* (1922)

The Realism of Proposals and Proposers

The third principle of foundation grantmaking is the importance of realistic grant proposals and proposers. Foundations have program interests which applicants must meet, and a proposal must "meticulously delineate" the purpose of the project, ensuring that it matches a foundation's goals (Townsend 1974). Among a foundation's first questions when evaluating a grant request are:

> Is this type of project an activity that fits within (our) program interest? Is the problem one that needs solution? Is the proposal soundly conceived to accomplish its stated objective? Is this trip really necessary? (Mayer 1972)

Once a proposal meets a foundation's interest, the foundation must assess the project's feasibility, one of the five most important grantmaking criteria identified by Townsend (1974). Although grant criteria are "often not explicit," foundations look for a "good idea, a workable plan (and) a realistic budget.... " (Odendahl and Boris 1983b). Adds Townsend (1974): Foundations must also evaluate "whether method 'A' can reasonably be expected to achieve intended result 'B'," while distinguishing between projects which are "articulately described but lack substance" and those which have "real or potential merit but ... suffer important defects" (Allen 1965).

The Realism of Project Goals

The realism of project goals is carefully assessed by foundations, although grantmakers appear to recognize the difficulty of predicting the feasibility of objectives. "Not all things worthwhile necessarily lend themselves to measurement," a foundation officer told Townsend (1974). "We tend to discount goals because they are usually set too high," said another officer. "I am usually sold on the objective, whether or not it can be achieved," adds a third. Reports Townsend: "Apparently fundors support projects in which reasonable results are expected, even when stated goals seem only partially achievable" (1974).

Johnson (1975a) addresses the realism of goals in a fictitious course for foundation grantees. Session three of the course is entitled "Coping with the Pressures of Goals" and discusses the

> evolution of goals from initial raw program idea through proposal stage, funding and actual practice.... How to recognize and deal with differences in goal perceptions between grantee and grantor, (especially) differences that do not surface until well into the funding period. Recognizing the perspective of those foundation people who give to goals, invest in the future and tend to live in and for the future; how to anticipate their difficulties in responding to your work when it become the present. How to change goals acceptably in light of program progress. Dealing with limited success and limited failure in the face of great expectations.

In the course's fourth session, Johnson (1975a) suggests ways of coping with the "pressures to be all things" by departing from the "Mr. Fixit Syndrome" in which applicants pledge to solve all parts of a problem and foundations readily accept the offer.

The Realism of Budgets

Foundations also closely inspect the budgets of grant proposals. Mayer's advice to grantseekers: "Have you examined the anticipated costs of your project in the most minute detail? Is your estimated budget as tight as it can be?" (1972) F. Lee and Barbara Jacquette explain that a realistic financing plan includes a statement of expected income with anticipated expenditures in logical categories. Soundness of the budget, report the authors, is an important grantmaking criterion: "Is it adequate for the job to be accomplished, but not so generous as to be wasteful?" (1973) Asking for too little money, according to Kimball (1974), is just as bad as asking for too much. "In either case it shows a lack of realistic planning and connotes fuzzy thinking (and) sloppy administration."

Goodwin (1976) believes that an "ill-conceived, unrealistic and vague" budget may reflect similar shortcomings in a proposed project. Moreover, an applicant's financial statement may disclose not only its financial position, but also its "administrative efficiency" (Allen 1965). A complex financial statement may reflect an obsolete organizational structure or ineffective operating procedures, while a simple report may indicate efficient management (Allen 1965). The financial statement may also disclose reserves so large that a foundation may decide that a grant is not needed.

The Realism of Form and Content

The format of proposals is also examined by grantmakers, and proposals range from "cheap mimeographed letters ... to gold-embossed brochures with expensive art work" (Andrews 1956). Some of these appeals come from hopeful individuals with a minimal knowledge of foundations. One grantseeker, however, reports "great success" with thirty brochures in "gold-plated imitation leather covers with illustrations (and) special printing. . . . " (Quay 1952). Smith, though, indicates that "real" ideas and programs are often funded, even if not in perfect proposal form. Conversely, "fancily garbed presentations" masking shallow content "do not impress anyone" (Smith 1979).

In evaluating content, foundations must separate carefully conceived proposals from the "superficial, the poorly planned, and (the) inconsequential" (Pattillo 1965). The variety of requests is broad, with purposes ranging from a study of "melting the polar ice caps" (Andrews 1956) to "irrigating the Sahara, the Sinai Peninsula, and Death Valley" (Goulden 1971). One foundation received requests to print a folder of religious sayings for servicemen, to promote "singing among boys" at naval training stations, and to "harvest the ideas and constructive thoughts of the American people" (Harrison and Andrews 1946). Foundations are frequent targets of a "lunatic fringe," reports Andrews (1956), persons who seek to abolish poverty at a stroke or invent perpetual motion machines. Such appeals, he confesses, are troublesome. The proposers are "earnest, dedicated, and exceedingly hard to shake off." Moreover, once in a while they might be right. A foundation would almost certainly have put Galileo in this class, with his strange idea of the earth moving around the sun (Andrews 1956). "Sometimes I wonder if we give enough attention to the really kooky ones," adds a foundation officer. "What would we have done . . . had a sailor walked in here five centuries ago and asked for money to make a voyage to prove the world is round?" (Goulden 1971).

The scope of grant requests may be bounded only by the imagination of the millions of Americans in the constituency of foundations. Goulden (1971) cites grant requests from

> an about-to-be-released convict who wanted a $10,000 annual stipend to prove that criminal instincts can be suppressed by a person in comfortable means; uncountable writers who were only a few thousand words . . . away from completing the Greatest American Novel; (and) students who thought society would benefit were they to complete another year of graduate school. . . .

Other grantseekers appear to misunderstand the purpose of foundations. A woman offered the Carnegie Corporation a "cookstove which is in good condition," while a man from India asked the Corporation to buy 100,000 monkeys yearly. Gardner, former President of the Corporation, said that some proposals had an "other-world quality." A man from Michigan wrote Gardner that he was in constant communication with "many spirits from beyond" including Andrew Carnegie, and that Carnegie endorsed his grant request. Another grantseeker claimed that he himself was Carnegie (Carnegie Corporation 1955). Macdonald (1956), who defined the Ford Foundation as a "large body of money surrounded on all sides by people who want some," laments the effect on proposals of the Foundation's relocation to New York. "We don't get the kind we used to in Pasadena," he reports, noting that the Foundation's staff called their California office "Itching Palms." Concludes Macdonald (1956): "The entertainment quality has fallen off."

CLARITY: THE FOURTH GRANTMAKING PRINCIPLE

Humpty Dumpty: "When I use a word, it means just what I choose it to mean—neither more nor less."

Alice: "The question is whether you can make words mean so many different things."

Lewis Carroll, *Alice in Wonderland*

Each year, foundations receive thousands of proposals from educational, social, medical, and service institutions. In 1987, the Ford Foundation alone received 17,000 proposals and inquiries for grants, and among all foundations, grant requests are increasing in number, magnitude, and the diversity of issues represented (*The Chronicle of Higher Education*, October 12, 1988; Higgins 1976).

Definitions of Grant Proposals

Perhaps the earliest definition of a grant proposal is from a 14th century administrative handbook for Cistercian monks which recommended that a proposal have five parts: "(i) a honeyed Salutation; (ii) a tactful Exordium (introduction); (iii) a Narration; (iv) a Petition; and (v) a Conclusion" (Phillips 1969). The monks also developed 22 letters of transmittal to introduce their proposals, citing such reasons for the desirability of philanthropy as "generosity in order to avoid ridicule," "the wealthy's obligation to give," "do as you would be done by," and "to be kind is better than being an animal."

Modern definitions of grant proposals include that of Gregg (1953), who believes that a proposal should: 1) define the problem and its significance; 2) present the qualifications of the people to lead the project; and 3) discuss the circumstances that favor undertaking the work. Pattillo (1962) adds that a proposal should describe the expected results of a project, and Lefferts concludes that a proposal is a representation of a program, a request, an instrument of persuasion, a promise, and a plan (1978).

The Mystery of Grant Proposals

Although grant proposals have simple elements, writing them is often perceived as "painful" (DeBakey 1977). "Madness" seems to overcome some people when they write proposals, reports McGuire (1981), even though "common sense" is a proposal's most important quality. There is nothing mystical about grant proposals. There are no "trade secrets or magical formulas;" an idea and a plan of action are the main requirements (Pattillo 1965). Barzun, however, with tongue in cheek, believes that grant proposals are mysterious, "a literary form" whose correct composition is an "art not vouchsafed to everyone." But Rusk (1961) considers such thinking a "myth," adding that there is no special way to apply to foundations. Says Rusk: foundations want to know what applicants plan to do in language that can be understood. The more fanciful the proposal, the "more immediate the skepticism" of the foundation (Rusk 1961).

The Importance of Clarity

As the competition for foundation funds intensifies, writing grant proposals (euphemistically called "grantsmanship" or worse, "resource procurement") becomes increasingly important because the quality of a proposal is a "critical factor, if not *the* critical factor" in obtaining a grant (Lefferts 1982).

Magat (1983) reviewed the grantmaking literature and interviewed foundation officers, finding that clarity is very important in proposals. Lefferts (1982) cites nine criteria by which foundations evaluate grant requests, and clarity is the first factor. "If I had to identify the most important literary requisite for grant applications," adds DeBakey (1977), "I would choose precision . . . in choice of words and in their . . . intended meaning." According to Wacaster, many proposals are flawed by weak purpose statements, resulting from poor writing or unclear goals. Such shortcomings are "red flags," for if an organization cannot clearly state its case, how will it be able to carry out a project? If the intent of a proposal is not clearly explained, adds Lobman, the idea "probably isn't clear in the first place" (Perry 1982). Dunham is even more direct: "If people can't write in English," the proposal is "probably not worth funding" (Perry 1982).

But what is judged in a proposal: writing skill or the ability to do the project? Both, says DeBakey (1977), and many foundations believe that the two are "inextricably related," for a "sloppily developed product" reflects the same kind of thinking. Elliott, a foundation trustee, believes that the need for clarity applies to foundations as well as applicants. Having read foundation reports of "meaningful interactions" and "tireless pursuits of excellence," Elliott urges program officers to improve their writing. Plain English, she says, can bring rewards other than board understanding; applicants will be able to tell "what you are interested in" (1984).

Brevity and Substance

Foundations are as critical of extremely long proposals as they are of vague writing. Although foundations do not judge applications solely by their brevity, proposals needing "reams and reams" of paper are probably weak (Pattillo 1965). "If you send a weighty proposal," warns McGuire (1981), foundations will not go to the trouble of discovering "what it is you have in mind." On the other hand, brevity may improve the chances that proposals will be read seriously, for "excess verbiage" often indicates a "deficiency of substance" (Broce 1979). In many cases, says Pattillo (1965), the theme of a proposal can be stated in three or four pages, and often the best requests can be reduced to "one paragraph."

> Without wishing to state this as an axiom, I can say that in almost every instance I have seen a voluminous proposal requiring a large amount of paper, the lack of brevity seemed to indicate that the drafters of the proposal could not see clearly the essentials of their plans (Pattillo 1965).

Grantseekers who use verbiage may be compensating for a lack of substance, and these applicants often yield the lowest return on a foundation's investment. Their work, says Pattillo (1965), is usually as "nebulous and hazy and inconclusive" as their propsals. Moreover, some professions ("I dare not name them," Pattillo confesses) are consumed with wordiness and jargon, unable to state even the least complicated ideas in simple English (1965).

Recommendations for Proposals

Many foundation officers who are critical of the clarity of grant proposals offer recommendations for improvement.

On the Structure of Proposals . . .

"Keep the written proposal short and clear. State at the outset what is to be accomplished, who expects to accomplish it, how much it will cost, and how long it will take" (F. Lee and Barbara Jacquette 1973).

"The proposal has to communicate quickly. . . . It has to be direct and to the point. You are much better off if you are concise" (McGuire 1981).

On Clarity . . .

"The proposal must be clearly written and organized so that it can be readily followed and easily understood. Complicated sentence structure, verbiage, abstractions (and) long sentences . . . should be avoided" (Lefferts 1982).

"There is no place for the elegant, descriptive prose of a *New Yorker* short story. The words to use in writing a proposal are the words that you use everyday (McGuire 1981).

On Jargon . . .

"The project or program should be concisely described . . . with a minimum of technical jargon" (Pattillo 1965).

"Any proposal that's full of a lot of jargon is automatically discarded" (Dunham in Perry 1982).

On Exaggeration . . .

"Cross out a few adjectives and adverbs" (McGuire 1981).

"(P)rogram officers are well informed. . . . They can spot overstatements quickly, and there is no doubt that such exaggeration has negative impact" (McGuire 1981).

"The successful applicant will have a number of qualities, which will probably not include modesty. . . . " (Whitaker 1974).

On Fancy Proposals . . .

"There is no need (for) leather binding with silver braid and gold lettering. This is just window dressing and it is not likely to impress an experienced foundation officer" (Pattillo 1965).

The literature on foundations is replete with calls for clarity in grant proposals. But despite such suggestions, many proposal writers use a language of exaggeration which I call "Proposalese."

Proposalese: The Grammar of Grantseekers

Proposalese is a flowery and funny language that uses big words to explain small ideas. Proposalese prefers the obscure to the familiar, the complex to the simple, and the long to the short. In short, Proposalese never says anything in short. In Proposalese, grantseekers do not merely get an idea; they "nourish a notion," "develop a concept," or "construct a conceptual framework." Why does no one have an idea anymore? asks Safire (1981). It's always a "concept," he says, which is an "idea with big ideas."

McGuire (1981), who read some 5,000 grant proposals while working at a large foundation, noticed a "universal proposal language" so similar that entire paragraphs could be switched from proposal to proposal. Three examples of Proposalese, "intellectual continuum," "perceptual parameter," and "developmental linkage," illustrate its first characteristic: Proposalese is prolific; its words are interchangeable. These three pieces of Proposalese easily become "perceptual continuum," "developmental parameter," "intellectual linkage," "developmental continuum," "perceptual linkage," or "intellectual parameter"—nine highly useful phrases in all.

The second characteristic of Proposalese is that it is purposely unclear. Much of social science, says Newman (1974), consists of "taking clear ideas and making them opaque." According to Macdonald (1956), the authors of a study on foreign students in American colleges worried that their report was not "perspicuous." The authors feared that the study was not clear. But did they use the word, clear? Of course not, they used perspicuous, an unclear word for clear.

The third characteristic of Proposalese is its self-indulgence; its most common words are "unique," "excellent," and "outstanding" (McGuire 1981). In Proposalese, all ideas are "unique," all programs are "excellent," and all results are "outstanding." Proposal writers do not merely raise money; they are "development officers," who turn "germinal but viable concepts" into "seminal opportunities" to "maximize the mileage" of "seed capital" so that grants will have a "multiplier effect" and "make the peaks higher" (Whitaker 1974).

The fourth characteristic of Proposalese is its versatility. Proposalese lends itself not only to the arts, sciences, and humanities, but even to sports. When watching a boxing match on TV, I turn down the volume on my set and call the action in Proposalese: "The Champion, moving quickly out of his corner, circles the ring using an 'innovative research methodology' to measure his opponent. The Kid, new to the rigors of the ring, counters with his own 'short-term programming pattern.' Dancing now, the Champ 'implements the learning process' with a combination of 'performance-oriented, competency-based' blows. Stunned, the Challenger falls, his 'cognitive and supportive human resources' expended."

"Unique," "excellent," and "outstanding" may be the most popular words in Proposalese, but nine words have been elected to the Proposalese Hall of Fame. The All-Star lineup:

Leading off and playing center field, the Georgia Peach, Ty Cognitive;
Playing second and batting second, Frankie Framework;
Playing first and batting third, the Iron Horse, Lou Generic;
Hitting cleanup and playing right field, Babe Rudiment;

Playing left field and batting fifth, Stan "The Man" Multidimensional;
Playing third and hitting sixth, Pie Programmatic;
Playing short and stroking seventh, Pee Wee Parameter;
Catching and batting eighth, Yogi Behavioral;
And pitching, the fireballing Dizzy Dialogue.

Some people from a small town once asked me to help them get a grant. Their entire proposal read: "We need $1,000 to fix our sidewalks." No Proposalese there. Unfortunately, I was unable to help; complex proposal guidelines (written naturally in Proposalese) soon frustrated the group. However, I did write the group's request in Proposalese, and my version of the proposal read: "As the legitimate representatives of a multi-ethnic, rural living unit, we seek an innovative and viable solution to the ills plaguing our community. Using an interdisciplinary strategy, we have identified our target area and have established a sound relational analysis of the operational parameters of our dilemma. Our estimated five-year allocation of $250,000 represents a minimal commitment to the development of an on-going program which will spawn a national demonstration model. If such an endeavor is consistent with your philosophical attunement, we shall enjoy the opportunity to engage in a meaningfully joint evaluative dialogue together with you." One lady in the group best evaluated my version of their proposal: "Too many baloney," she said.

Foundationese

Proposalese is not the only jargon in philanthropy; foundations have one, too, which Macdonald (1956) calls "Foundationese." Like Latin, Foundationese is a dead language, written rather than spoken, designed for ceremony rather than utility. Foundationese is an "esoteric language" whose purpose is not to communicate or give information, but to reassure everyone that everything is well in hand. Foundationese is committee language, ever seeking the lowest common denominator, a point which is often "well below sea level" (Macdonald 1956).

The first characteristic of Foundationese is its mastery of the obvious; Foundationese cannot bear not to repeat ideas that do not bear repeating. From an annual report of the Ford Foundation: "The Foundation attempts to administer its funds in ways that strengthen its grantees and enhance their ability to accomplish the purposes for which the grants were made." Are readers to conclude, asks Macdonald (1956), that the Foundation pursues this policy instead of trying to *weaken* grantees and *lessen* their ability to achieve the aims of the grants? In 1950, the Ford Foundation said it would "support activities designed to secure greater allegiance to the basic principles of freedom and democracy in the solution of the insistent problems of an ever changing society." Instead, asks Brown (1965), of funding revolution, encouraging totalitarianism, or *ignoring* problems in society?

The second characteristic of Foundationese is its self-righteousness. According to Nielsen (1972), the Irvine Foundation of California issued no annual report before the mid-1960s, and its President said the Foundation's policy was to offer no public information. In 1965, "evidently as a result of growing criticism" (Nielsen 1972), the Foundation issued its first public report. Financial data were omitted, but the Foundation nobly (and self-righteously) explained that it "fulfills its public trust by exercising its intrinsic advantages of independence and flexibility and by utilization of its capacity to provide timely financial assistance to the solution of critical problems and to relieve acute wants and needs of the people of California." The Foundation apparently believed that this statement would reduce public suspicion.

The third characteristic of Foundationese is its reversibility. From an annual report of the Ford Foundation:

1. "The Trustees of the Ford Foundation believe that a healthy economy is essential if American democracy is to function effectively;" and
2. "The Ford Foundation believes that the advancement of human welfare depends on the partnership in progress of all free men."

"Like a trench coat," explains Macdonald (1956), these two sentences are reversible, thus: "Democracy is essential if a healthy economy is to function effectively" and "The partnership in progress of all free men depends on the advancement of human welfare." Says Macdonald (1956): "Gives just as good wear either way."

The fourth characteristic of Foundationese is its similarity to Proposalese; foundations render "behavioral responses" to grantseekers who request "flexible definitions." Grantseekers may use Proposalese because they think foundations expect it. "The proverbial joke about the X Foundation" is that the proposal with the best chance of funding is the one with the "most impenetrable jargon" (Whitaker 1974). Nonetheless, grantseekers must take Foundationese seriously ("despite its appearance to the contrary") and show proper concern for "changing fluxes," "ongoing interfaces," and "self-liquidating leverages" (Whitaker 1974). As a foundation officer told Whitaker: "In our world, you have to have leverage even to get out of bed in the morning" (1974).

Proposalese and Foundationese are only part of a larger assault on English by education, government, business, and the media. American English, which was once rich, now has euphemism, redundancy, and overblown expressions.

The Deterioration of English

Today, used cars are "pre-owned," garbagemen are "sanitary engineers," and scrappy athletes are "opportunistic." Rain is "precipitation" and clouds "encroach," "crescendo a bit," or "develop into enhanced cloudiness." Taxes are "revenue enhancements," Life Savers are "mints," and life jackets are "personal flotation devices."

An American intercontinental ballistic missile is called the "Peacekeeper," and the Pentagon defines the neutron bomb as a "radiation enhancement weapon." The CIA did brainwashing experiments at its "Society for the Investigation of Human Ecology." The U.S. Navy underestimated the number of Cubans on Grenada, saying, "We were not micromanaging Grenada intelligencewise until about that timeframe."

Eastern Airlines provides "sortation" of baggage after passengers "deplane." Amtrak trains "platform" at their destinations, but in bad weather, service may be "annulled." A representative of Pennsylvania's Three Mile Island nuclear power plant called the accident there a "normal aberration." After the accident, the chairman of the Nuclear Regulatory Commission said it would be "prudent to consider expeditiously the provision of instrumentation that would provide an unambiguous indication of the level of fluid in the reactor vessel." One can only imagine what he would have said had there been a complete meltdown.

The weakening of English has created two other jargons, Educationese, the language of "textbooks, official documents (and) commencement speeches" (Barzun 1944), and a second language that I call "Redundancese."

Educationese: The Expression of Educators

In Educationese, students are "talented," faculty are "dedicated," and administrators are invariably "effective." Research may be either "multidimensional" or "multidisciplinary," but objectives must always be "measurable." Libraries are "learning resource centers," lessons are "interactive intellectual modules," and computers are "individualized instructional implements." Questions in classrooms create "hypothetical learning modes," enabling "transpersonal teaching" to yield "expected student outcomes." Failing this, teachers may have to get tough and use "stepwise regression strategies."

Educationese is the preferred tongue of academic committees, and at one such committee, the following exchange was overheard:

"Our objective," said the chair, "is to develop a commonality to guide behavioral learning."

"Pardon me," interrupted the political science professor, "we need some operational definitions before we problem-solve."

"I agree," said the psychology instructor. "We can't do a thing without a cognitive framework."

"You're right," said the chair. "Let's initiate implementation. I think we have commonality."

A college administrator who praised a workshop for its "pyramid of contributions" also said the seminar was not a "panacea for all our problems." (Perhaps its "primordial thrust" failed because of poor "commensurate model analysis.") According to Macdonald (1956), one study claimed that it could document "varieties of cross-cultural experience," but could not state "firm conclusions about causes and effects." Explains Macdonald: the study did not find anything. Another study proposed a major review of "problems discerned in the initial phase of research." Translation: "We're starting the whole thing all over" (Macdonald 1956).

A Massachusetts company advertised for a "Conceptual Thinker/ Generalist," no doubt for one of the firm's upper levels. The San Francisco Art Institute, which advertised for a Dean, anticipated the dangers of Educationese. Its ad asked candidates to submit a statement of their "educational philosophy," which the Institute wisely defined as "what you think an art school should be" (*The Chronicle of Higher Education*, November 5, 1986; August 4, 1982).

Redundancese: "The Spread of Nuclear Proliferation"

Educationese is not the only jargon contributing to the deterioration of English; Redundancese also bears responsibility. Redundancese is characterizied by redundancies; i.e., using more words than necessary. For example, when banks offer "free gifts," they are redundant—all gifts are free, or they would not be gifts. When florists sell "bouquets of flowers," they are also redundant, for all bouquets are of flowers. Plumbers, too, are redundant when they fix "hot water heaters." What other kind of water would a water heater heat?

In Redundancese, fashionable clothing stores are "truly unique," "singularly unique," "especially unique," and "now even more unique." Tax evaders submit "falsely padded" expense accounts, acting under "false pretenses." Patients undergo "delicate heart surgery" and emerge in "extremely critical" condition. Police seek "positive identification" of "alleged suspects" who commit "senseless murders."

Newspapers hire "investigative reporters," television shows are "pre-recorded," and radio stations play old songs to evoke "past nostalgia." To news broadcasters, every world hotspot is a "serious dilemma," a "major crisis," or a "major crisis situation." ABC television said that it would cover Iran as long as the "crisis remains critical" and ABC Radio warned of the danger of disease in Armenia from "dead corpses." United Press International was not content that Tip O'Neill was the heir apparent to House Speaker Carl Albert. To UPI, Tip was the "apparent heir apparent" (Newman 1975).

In international affairs, negotiations begin with "opening gambits" seeking a "consensus of opinion" on "legitimate rights." Diplomats meet in "close proximity" to discuss "other alternatives," the "end result" of which is sometimes a "successful solution." In 1983, American and Soviet negotiators accepted a "double build-down" plan to reduce nuclear weapons (*Time*, October 17, 1983). Nevada Senator Chic Hecht demonstrated his opposition to nuclear arms by rejecting a nuclear waste "suppository" for his state (*Time*, October 24, 1988). For another United States Senator, though, slowing nuclear proliferation was not enough; he urged Congress to control the "spread of nuclear proliferation" (Newman 1979).

CONTINUITY: THE FIFTH GRANTMAKING PRINCIPLE

"No permanent good could be anticipated by giving aid for any purpose that was incapable of provoking a desire on the part of the recipient to assist and carry it forward."

> "Memorandum on Principles"
> The Rockefeller Foundation
> Raymond B. Fosdick
> *The Story of the Rockefeller
> Foundation* (1952)

" 'Tis not enough to help the feeble up
But to support him after."

> William Shakespeare
> *Timon of Athens*,I,1,107

The Continuity of Grant Programs

The fifth grantmaking principle emphasizes the importance of the continuity of grant programs, an issue which has received considerable attention in the literature on foundations. In 1930, Embree defined the grantmaking philosophy of foundations as "giving as little as possible for as short a time as possible," while the Rockefeller Foundation's original policy statement said, "Outside agencies should not become permanent or indefinite charges." Weaver (1967) evaluates proposed programs on their potential "continuity and stability," for as Whitaker (1974) explains, foundations are reluctant to become the "sole, or even the major" source of an organization's support. When considering a grant, Mayer (1972) examines how a project will be financed beyond its "immediate grant period," noting that grantseekers often claim that programs will be self-sufficient by the end of their grants. However, reports Mayer (1972), "Seldom, in my experience, have these estimates been realistic."

Grantseekers are not alone in optimistic predictions of the self-sufficiency of grant programs. Some foundations believe that an organization "touched by (their) magic wand" receives an "infusion of vigor," soon becoming "self-reliant and a recognized element of the community" (Goulden 1971). However, contends Goulden (1971), many grantees "couldn't become self-supporting unless they robbed banks." A Bush Foundation study may support his claim. The foundation surveyed rejected applicants from 1973 to 1983 to determine the effect of denials on proposed programs. Reports Archabel (1984): " . . . approximately one-fourth of the denied proposals were abandoned entirely after denial . . . 22% in 1973 (N = 41), 21% in 1977 (N = 33), and 23% in 1983 (N = 39)." Moreover, foundations themselves may damage the potential continuity of grant programs. "I think we all (have made a grant) for a particular project that is to run 'X' months or a year," explains May. "After we do this we find out that maybe we've done more harm than good."

> Staff is hired, and then they come to the end of the grant period, and they haven't gotten any other money, and the staff has to be let go, and the expectations they've raised . . . have to be dropped. It's really a pretty irresponsible thing that we've done (May in Kennedy 1977).

Macdonald (1956) adds that grants can increase growth too suddenly, causing institutions to expand "out of all proportion" to their normal rate of development. "The first thing you know," he reports, "you have an organizational cancer." But Weaver (1967) believes that it is difficult for foundations to avoid responsibility for continuing support, even though "prudent foundations," according to Macdonald (1956), try to disabuse grantees of this "illusion." Unless a recipient is "weaned," writes Macdonald (1956), "he will never learn to forage for himself."

Grantees, however, also bear a major responsibility for the continuity of projects. "If a new program is ultimately going to place a burden on an institution's already tight budget, that reality had best be faced honestly before the proposal goes to a foundation" (Landau 1975). By taking a grant, adds Barzun, an organization incurs expenses which are "bound to increase" (Goulden 1971). Barzun saw a $34,000 research grant grow to $500,000 five years after its grant expired. Concludes Barzun: "Stopping the growth of a well-nourished research project is as difficult as rooting out crabgrass" (Goulden 1971).

Although grantees have a responsibility for the continuity of programs, foundations are especially wary of long-term commitments to the same recipients. Such grants violate one of the "sound principles" of foundations, to be "alert for the new and innovative." Explains Friedman (1973):

> In theory . . . one of the great strengths of private foundations is their flexibility. . . . Unlike government, private foundations usually do not allocate funds more than one year in advance. They are free to develop new programs without being locked into prior funding commitments.

"What hardening of the arteries is to the human body," explains Macdonald (1956), "getting loaded up with future commitments is to a foundation." The problem is most acute with institutions which receive a grant one year and "assume that they will get one the next. . . . " Because foundations like to "do a job and get out," the extent to which they are involved in continuing support is a "measure of the degree to which they tie up their own initiative" (Kimball 1974). Adds Freeman (1981):

> Project grants . . . give the grantmaker maximum flexibility to move to other . . . program areas when a project is completed. The project grant has the advantage of an agreed cut-off date beyond which the foundation has no commitment.

According to Freeman (1981), foundations seldom make grants for "longer periods than three years." "We look at a project very hard in the third year," says one foundation officer, "(and) it's considerably more difficult to get money to continue past that point than it is to receive the initial grant" (Goulden 1971). Welling thinks that foundations should fund projects for a "maximum of four or five years. If it takes longer for a project to prove its worth, the project is worthless" (Whitaker 1974). However, asks a foundation official, "How can you impose a three-year limit on a search for the cure for cancer? A scientist who knows he must stop every two or three years and begin that awful search for money doesn't focus his full attention on the research" (Goulden 1971). "Aren't these limits arbitrary standards based neither on excellence nor on urgent public needs?" asks Eisenberg (1983).

> Are they not frequently a denial of innovation and risk-taking? Put another way, might it not be more productive, innovative and cutting-edge to support on a long-term basis organizations that make a significant difference?

Some foundations deride the "pensioners" who rely on them for continuing support. Says one foundation officer:

> I feel that a scientist or researcher who comes back to the same foundation year after year, and always receives what he wants, gets into the psychological frame-of-mind that allows him to drag out his work indefinitely, to go down promising rabbit trails rather than stick to the business at hand (Goulden 1971).

However, says another official, "Don't be misled by those high-sounding statements about 'pensioners.' Much of it results from the fact that grant officers have a low threshold of boredom. They see the same name come up a few times, and what . . . excited them two years ago now seems commonplace. . . . " (Goulden 1971). Foundation staff need to "justify their existence," adds Whitaker (1974), and when grants are "tied up in long-term commitments," staff may begin to feel redundant.

Johnson (1975a) addresses the principle of continuity in his fictitious course on the "natural life cycle of funded programs." Topics in the course include the

> initial inspiration of a program idea, the period of gestation and articulation, the grant description as an illusion of program success, temptations of early limited victories, the crisis when you achieve a long-awaited plateau of program activity, the decision to go on, the decision to wind down, the decision to give the program away to somebody else.

To shorten their commitment to grantees, some foundations are reducing annual payments in the last years of multi-year awards. Other foundations insist that fund raising be a part of all projects, a policy which may create a "chill wind . . . on the necks of the grantees, stimulating them to raise money elsewhere" (Macdonald 1956). Explains O'Connell (1982):

> (Foundations) recognize that in the past their exclusive emphasis on funding program activities left (grantees) with limited time and funds

to try to build the funding capacity to continue these activities in the long-term. They recognize that they have had a major part in pushing these organizations into the arms of government—who else had enough money to carry on all of these pilot projects?

Thibault (1973), who studied grant programs in universities, uses the terms, "hard" and "soft" money, to emphasize the importance of the continuity principle.

Hard money . . . comes in year after year, based upon a tax base; capital that a university has that generates money for salaries (from) tuition income. . . . Soft money I call *funny money* because you come by it almost capriciously, after much hard work.

Because "soft" money can disappear at "almost any time," managing an institution is difficult when financial policies are decided in foundations or the government (Thibault 1973).

Too much soft money means that the university loses control of its staff. Too much soft money means that professors are not available for work with students—the professor will either be justifying his next grant, evaluating someone else's grant or will be at a meeting. . . . (Thibault 1973)

"Too much soft money," contends Thibault (1973), "makes for a staff of nervous wrecks." Thibault (1973) believes that all grantees, but especially colleges and universities, should answer several questions before accepting grants:

Can we take this money without compromising the university, its faculty or students? If all soft money was cut off tomorrow, could we still have a university; meaning—what effect on the life and the excellence of the academic community does the total soft money on this campus have?

Hollis (1938) notes that the continuity principle also requires decisions by foundations.

How far ahead shall future income be pledged to specific undertakings? What factors should determine the size of a grant to a given organization? Should the policy for payments on long-time grants be a uniformly increasing or decreasing sum? When and how should a foundation withdraw from a project to which it is making grants?

Despite efforts by foundations to answer such questions, Hollis (1938) reports that there is "no easy way" of withdrawing from projects that have been supported for years. Explains Hollis (1938): "No policy has yet been evolved that is an answer to the question." Nonetheless, Hollis (1938) believes that institutions should accept grants only when they match the work to which they are committed. The wisdom of this policy, he writes, is "every day more evident"

(1938). Concludes Kimball (1974): "Many a long journey begins with a single step. But many a long journey is never completed because the steps fail to continue."

TRUST: THE SIXTH GRANTMAKING PRINCIPLE

"Someone once said that a foundation executive is a friend who stabs you in the front. Would that it were true."

> Orville Brim
> "Do We Know What We Are
> Doing?"
> *The Future of Foundations* (1973)

"It is what we are willing to do for foundation money, not what foundations want or ask us to do, that makes foundation giving a social and governmental menace."

> William H. Allen
> *Rockefeller: Giant, Dwarf, Symbol*
> (1930)

The Partnership of Grantor and Grantee

The sixth grantmaking principle concerns the necessity of trust between grantmakers and grantseekers, a quality on which all other grantmaking principles depend. The principle of trust may originate in the difference between giving and grantmaking. To give is to transfer something from one person to another. To make a grant, however, is to respond to a request which the grantor may reject. The term, grant, therefore, connotes a "two-way obligation" (Hertz and Kurzig 1983).

The relationship of grantor and grantee is "subtle and sensitive," for the requirements of a foundation must be balanced with the independence of a grantee (Hertz and Kurzig 1983). The Council on Foundations (1980 and 1984) encourages grantors and grantees to recognize their "community of interest" and to develop a relationship of "mutual respect, candor, and understanding." Freeman (1981) urges grantors and grantees to nurture their partnership, noting that both parties can contribute to the relationship. Foundations can provide "more than money;" they can help prepare grant applications and identify other sources of funding. Grantees can bring "enthusiasm and dedication," as well as a degree of knowledge "which the foundation 'generalist' can rarely match." Miller (1984) encourages foundations to "stand in the shoes" of grantseekers, for both parties are "interdependent as to ideas." Joseph (1986d) believes that foundations have a "special responsibility" to strengthen the partnership, and he urges grantors to "feel more directly the emotional effects of the transaction."

Achieving partnership between grantor and grantee, however, may be the most difficult element of grantmaking. Although the literature supports the importance of partnership between grantor and grantee, their relationship is "all too often" like one between a "banker and a borrower" (Joseph 1986d). "A fundamental human connection is not likely to be made," explains Joseph (1986e), for although funds may change hands, "full participation in the underlying concerns of the two parties" rarely occurs. Partnership may be hindered by one of the "greatest evils" in grantmaking, the "resistance to intimacy."

> Much of the structure of philanthropy mitigates against knowing the recipient; he or she may be of a different nation, class, or culture and the foundation's structure is intended ideally to bridge this gap. . . . Unfortunately, the bridge often becomes a wall (Crawshaw and Bruce 1978).

If mutual respect does not link grantor with grantee, "the whole thing is a sham," claims Menninger (1981). Moreover, the refusal to develop the relationship can reduce grantmaking to being "crass, manipulative or mechanistic" or to be characterized by "plain seductions or aggressive acts" (Menninger 1981). Therefore, in the relationship of grantor and grantee, there is "some virtue (and) some meanness of spirit, but mostly a large grey area of ignorance and uncertainty" (Eisenberg 1983).

Money is the heart of the relationship of grantor and grantee, and its influence can be good or "downright vicious" (Weaver 1967).

> We see money as a way of buying love, or appreciation, or approbation. We can see it as a way out of dependency and a means of becoming autonomous. Money can be power to control others, or to get revenge. Money . . . often distorts relationships (and) when it is used to buy and control relationships, (it) ultimately demeans them. . . . (Menninger 1981)

Money is often equated with worth. "We use . . . dollars to characterize ultimate value," explains Menninger (1981). "The phrase 'net worth' states the value of the individual. And we honestly do believe that the larger the number, the 'more valuable'—and somehow 'better'—the individual is."

> By an insidious transformation we convert quantity into quality. On reflection, most of us do acknowledge that there is no necessary rela-

tionship; indeed, we can often see inverse relationships between quantity of money and quality of life, whether we're talking about individuals or institutions.

Because people will do almost anything for money, it can "warp beyond repair" colleges, universities, agencies, and even churches, "for what minister will knowingly offend his wealthiest parishoner?" (Kimball 1974)

Violations of Trust by Foundations

Foundations violate the principle of trust when they are arrogant with grantseekers or less than candid when rejecting proposals. Among the indignities suffered by grantseekers at the hands of foundations are unreturned telephone calls, no responses to letters, the inability to obtain information about pending proposals, waiting "many months or over a year" for grant decisions, the inability to meet with foundation representatives, rude treatment by foundation officers, and "no reasons . . . for turndowns of grant proposals" (Eisenberg 1983). Such practices indicate that grantseekers "are not equal" in the philanthropic process, but rather, are relegated to "second class citizenship" (Eisenberg 1983). Odendahl and Boris (1983b) note that prompt acknowledgment of proposals and early decisions on grant requests may improve the partnership of grantor and grantee. However, report Crossland and Trachtenberg (1982), many grantseekers have experienced the frustration of submitting a proposal only to discover "a year later" that it was rejected while they waited in "prayerful anticipation." Broughton (1965) contends that foundations must improve their integrity and honesty, noting that some foundations are

> so ill-staffed, so small in resources, so responsive to personal whim . . . so without a demonstrated public service program, that they are deplorable. . . . Certainly, it would be helpful . . . if legal quackeries masquerading as foundations were eliminated.

Examples of abuses by foundations include the Julius S. Eaton Education Foundation, which was established to make "interest-free loans to needy students" at the University of Miami. The true purpose of the foundation, however, was recruiting players for the university's football team. The St. Genevieve Foundation supported twin sisters through "several years of parties and gay living."

> One of the twins lived in a posh duplex (and) spent more than $3,000 on clothes one year. The other twin, esconced in a five-bedroom mansion on Lake Oswego, was paid $36,000 as a 'caretaker of the house'. . . . (The founder of the St. Genevieve Foundation said) he

needed companionship and knew no other way to obtain it. A jury convicted him of tax evasion (Goulden 1971).

The rejection of grant requests is another way in which foundations violate the principle of trust. Rejecting grant requests is a fact of foundation life, explains Freeman (1981), because for every grant awarded, there are "eight or ten rejected . . . not counting the form appeals." "Between 9:15 a.m. and noon," reports Goulden (1971), one foundation officer rejected "by phone, by letter, and in person" requests from

> (1) an Ivy League school that wanted the foundation to assume financial responsibility for a professional chair. . . . (2) a California college that decided the most efficacious way to revitalize its business school was to have the foundation buy it a computer; (3) another California college whose medical school had just learned that it would not be receiving expected money from the National Institute of Health . . . and wondered if the foundation would care to send out some dollars to fill the chink in its budget; and (4) nine other institutions whose applications acquired the fatal endorsement, 'outside program scope'. . . .

Most applications must be rejected because they are "out of program, they are mediocre or worse, or funds are simply not available" (Andrews 1956). The manner of rejection, however, is important. If roleplaying were part of the education of foundations, contends Freeman (1981), every foundation should be required to play the rejected applicant. "Only then would it be clear that how a foundation manager says 'no' is as important as why that decision is reached." The Council on Foundations (1984) believes that applicants whose proposals are beyond the interests of a foundation should be told "immediately," while grantseekers with requests under consideration should be informed of the "steps and timing (leading to) the final decision." Andrews (1956), however, believes that it is "seldom desirable" to explain the reason for rejecting a proposal, especially if the project seems "inadequate, unimportant, or even completely unworthy." Such a judgment, he notes, might be wrong, and the applicant will rarely accept the criticism. Barnard notes that some rejected applicants try to save self-respect by criticizing foundation decisions. However, he adds, there is "nothing you can do about it because you cannot tell people why you do not give them money" (U.S. House of Representatives, 1952). It is better to appear "stupid ourselves," said Keppel, than to make applicants feel that they have been "silly" (Andrews 1956). Weaver (1965) recommends that a rejection be cast in "perfectly spherical, polished form, with no protuberances that can be grabbed hold of to be thrown back" at the foundation for reconsideration. If a foundation indicates a flaw in a proposal, the applicant will write back with the "glad tidings" that the shortcoming has been corrected, asking the foundation to "please send the check by return mail." Foundations, therefore, are sometimes "less than truthful and substantially less than candid" when rejecting proposals.

> The usual commentary on a rejected proposal is evasive, philanthropic doubletalk that avoids the real reasons for the rejection: 'We have nothing but praise for your proposal . . . ' or 'We shall waste no time in reading it . . . ' When it is clear that the applicant is out of his depth (or is) proposing work that he or she is incompetent to do, then the (foundation) owes the applicant a direct answer and comment on that fact (Brim 1973).

"A friend (who) used to judge music competitions (said that) he wished he had a big rubber stamp that said, 'Give up!' This may be too rough, but it moves in the right direction" (Brim 1973).

Zurcher (1972), however, argues that foundations have a "moral if not a legal obligation" to explain why they accept some proposals and reject others, even if grantseekers must be told that they are less capable or less well-supported than others who receive grants.

> Such reasons for discriminating among applicants, alas, do exist. . . . In any event, honesty need not oust tact. Both are virtues; and a greater supply of each of them could be exploited profitably when a foundation says 'no' (Zurcher 1972).

May, however, indicates that rejections are inevitable.

> Of 20 proposals that are considered . . . 15 or 18 may be good, but only three are granted. So . . . if you grant the three you shouldn't think of the other 12 or 15 as being turned down. It's just that there had to be a choice made and some others were a little better and you chose those.

"If you can get that across to a grant seeker, and you usually can't," says May, "the relationship's a little better" (Kennedy 1977). Johnson (1976) offers two "handy form letters" for rejecting grant requests:

> (1) There is a real conflict of interest between the intent of your application and some economic or social conditions in the lives of those who run this foundation. There's a risk of either losing money or being embarrassed or both. . . . (2) Your proposal is for work that really makes us feel uncomfortable. We don't know much about it, but we just don't feel we want to have anything to do with it.

Weaver (1967), who considered one proposal "utterly irrelevant" to a foundation's interests, was confronted by the applicant, who demanded a hearing. Wrote Weaver:

> I think I ought to say to you at once that the project which you have in mind lies so completely outside of the program and policy of (this foundation) that there would be really no point in your discussing it with any of the officers here. . . . I am sorry to send you this disappointing reply.

The applicant, however, considered Weaver's letter "rude, insulting and infantile in its concept" and complained to the chairman of the foundation's trustees. Observes Weaver (1967):" 'The fury of a woman scorned' can sometimes be matched by the outrage of an applicant turned down."

Institutions which receive grants, however, are not necessarily "grateful or admiring," for many feel that they were "merely given their due" (Nielsen 1972). Whitaker (1974) adds that most grantees wish they had been given more; while others, who "usually sense that they perhaps have been given more than they deserve," may lose respect for grantmakers. Foundations must therefore expect something "both rewarding and punishing" in grantmaking. Ingratitude, ambivalence, or even envy are not unusual from recipients, especially once the "initial burst of gratitude" has subsided and the jealously that the grantee must receive while the foundation gives is realized (Crawshaw and Bruce 1978). Moreover, because the decision-making methods of foundations are rarely revealed, applicants may become "cynical about the entire process." When rejecting proposals, therefore, Freeman (1981) encourages foundations to remember that philanthropy is a "team operation." Responses to grantseekers should be "prompt and courteous, and should reflect the partnership concept. Too often," concludes Freeman (1981), "this is not the case."

Violations of Trust by Grantseekers

The tactics of some grantseekers reflect the "seamy side" of philanthropy (Hollis 1938) and range from "inaction, disgust and resignation" to the "agitated restlessness . . . of political revolution" (Crawshaw and Bruce 1978). Although the relationship of grantor and grantee is portrayed as a partnership, "adversarial elements also embrace the process" (Magat 1983a). The applicant is "after something the foundation has," so grantseeking can be a contest of "skills, if not wills." Although foundations may direct the grantmaking process, grantseekers are not "passive onlooker(s)" (Magat 1983a).

The questionable practices of grantseekers range from "mild wheedling" and cajolery to "wholesome pressure-group methods (and) anything short of murder" (Hollis 1938). Grantseekers can also demonstrate "hypocritical or offensive" behavior, assume aggressive postures, or issue "gushy praise." Bravado sometimes masks disdain, and contempt for foundations is common, especially when proposals are rejected (Menninger 1981). Grantseekers, however, may earn the mistrust of foundations, for the ranks of fundraisers include "too many snake-oil salesmen—those suntanned fellows with straight white teeth" who name-drop endlessly as they tell "hilarious anecdotes from summer cocktail parties on the Cape with this one from Ford, or that one from Rockefeller" (Landau 1975). "All these sharks have one thing in common. They see themselves as manipulators, and the foundation officers as the manipulated" (Landau 1975).

Asking for money, however, is difficult and reflects the "complex nature of the transaction between seeker and donor" (Menninger 1981).

> (T)he pursuit of funds often puts the seeker in the role of having to appeal to another for help, a position that sometimes feels like begging. . . . Asking implies need (but) need also implies inadequacy, and having to ask someone to meet this need exposes one . . . to feeling patronized and even depreciated. . . . (Menninger 1981)

"Getting money," adds Menninger (1981), "seems active and aggressive," while receiving money implies a "polite form of passive acceptance." Some grantseekers view the process as a "game with winners and losers and a score to keep," contending that "tricks and surprise tactics" are therefore allowable.

"How do you know . . . that you haven't been deliberately blindsided?" asks Kennedy (1977). "You mean conned?" replies May. "You don't. And you get conned all the time."

> I'm sure I know some people who aren't going to put it all out on the table. I know some that I'm going to give the fishy eye to them every single time and try and find out just what the hell it is they're hiding, because I know it's something (May in Kennedy 1977).

Sometimes we encounter an "oily creature" who insults us by assuming that we wished to be "fawned upon," adds Weaver (1967). On the other hand, "abnormally shy individuals," determined not to be "supplicant(s)," can sometimes exhibit "no other behavior but rudeness" (Weaver 1967). Another abuse by grantseekers is sending the same proposal to many foundations at the same time, a practice which may be both unethical and embarrassing.

> I recall a proposal that was submitted by a respected university to two foundations simultaneously and resulted in two grants. The administration was in the awkward position of having to apologize and decline one of the grants. The circumstances were almost such as to raise ethical questions (Pattillo 1965).

In 1965, Pattillo predicted the development of a code of ethics for educational fundraising, noting that many institutions were engaging in practices unworthy of higher education.

> I am entirely sympathetic with hard-pressed administrators who have the almost impossible task of finding sufficient money to finance their institutions. . . . But I still believe that the manipulative attitude toward donors, which is all too prevalent, is doing something to the dignity of college and university administration.

In 1922, Pritchett observed the effect of fundraising on college presidents.

> (The) wholesale college begging of the last twenty years (has transformed) the American college president into a soliciting agent. Scholarly men today hesitate to take the place of the college president (for) many find themselves . . . very much as the ass with the bundle of oats held just far enough in advance of his nose to keep him perpetually seeking to reach it.

"I suspect that there is many an administrator," adds Pattillo (1965), "who would be a little ashamed to confide even to his wife some of the tricky practices he has used to get money. . . . "

Johnson (1975a) proposes a course for foundation grantees called, "Where Hustling Ends and Trust Begins." In the fictitious course, he quotes a book called *Centering*, whose author discussed resistances against trust. Although the book is about teaching adults, Johnson (1975b) notes its applicability to grantseekers.

> I find that my principal task . . . is to win their trust. They tend to be overwhelmingly oriented to manipulation and to effect. It rarely occurs to them to work in a direct way with what they know and are. Their primary motivations are to please, to make a strong impression, to do either what is expected (if they are docile) or what is unexpected (if they are hostile). They assume that pretense and falsity are virtues. The whole thing sometimes seems like a massive confidence game.

"If this seems patronizing," asks Johnson (1975b), "turn it around, so that a grantee is saying this about a foundation person. 'It rarely occurs to them to work in a direct way with what they are . . . ' I've heard that said about us." Observes Johnson (1975b):

> We all know people . . . in this business who reach the ultimate state of cynicism where one guy schemes and lies to raise money and the other guy tries to catch him at it (if he's hostile) or just lies back and enjoys it (if he's docile).

Such transactions may be the worst in the relationship of foundations and grantseekers. "What terrible tricks we do get into," concludes Johnson (1975b), "in the ceremonies of giving and getting money."

VII

SUMMARY AND RECOMMENDATIONS

SUMMARY OF FINDINGS

Chapter One: A Synthesis of the Literature
on Foundations

The decline of foundation support of higher education and the lack of research on foundations indicate the need for a synthesis of the literature on foundations for higher education administrators. From 1970 to 1986, the foundations' share of voluntary support to higher education fell 15 percent, and foundations, which led all private donors to the academy from 1949 to 1969, now rank fourth behind alumni, friends, and corporations, outpacing only the religious denominations and consortia.

Lack of information on foundations has been a problem reported by a half-century of scholars, foundation executives, and higher education officers ranging from Lester (1935) to Payton (1985). Plinio (1986), President of the Prudential Foundation, indicates that "little is known and understood" about foundations, while Boris (1985), Vice President of Research for the Council on Foundations, believes that the need for research on foundations is "more compelling with every passing year." Read, Vice President of the Foundation Center, adds that the "low level" of understanding of foundations is "one of the biggest constant challenges we face" (Desruisseaux 1986e). Recent scholars including Boris (1985), Nielsen (1985), Plinio (1986), and Read (Desruisseaux 1986e) contend that the lack of information on foundations contributes to higher education's poor understanding of foundations and impedes the academy from constructively replying to the decrease in foundation aid. Academic leaders such as Bernstein, Bunting, Kerr, and Newman have commented on the failure of higher education to respond to the decline of foundation aid, and Payton, former Director of the Exxon Education Foundation, contends that the higher education disciplines have "sort of gone off and isolated themselves" (Sleeper 1985). Foundation officials including Hamburg of the Carnegie Corporation, Furman of the MacArthur Foundation, Sawyer of the A. W. Mellon Foundation, and Stanley of the Ford Foundation have also noted higher education's weak reply to the decrease in foundation aid. Higher education researchers including Cheit and Lobman (1979) and Broce (1981) believe that higher education's relationship with foundations has not only changed, but has deteriorated.

Foundations and Higher Education Income

Among the private donors to higher education, perhaps none has had greater influence than foundations. The grants of foundations helped produce standards for courses and credits, develop faculty pensions, construct facilities, conduct research, increase salaries, and expand educational opportunities for women and blacks.

The contributions of foundations to higher education are remarkable in light of the relatively small sums involved. Even at the peak of their grants to the academy, between 1915 and 1920 when large awards were made for capital purposes, foundation grants represented "no more than 10 percent" of the income of colleges and universities (Cheit and Lobman 1979). Although foundations may once have provided a tenth of higher education income, they now contribute a much smaller share of current funds. Between 1950 and 1985, foundation grants averaged just 1.7 percent of the current fund income of colleges and universities and declined from a high of nearly 3 percent in 1959–60 to 1.2 percent in 1984–85 (*Financial Statistics of Institutions of Higher Education*, selected years).

Foundations and Voluntary Support

Foundations have long been a major source of voluntary support of higher education. Between 1950 and 1986, foundations provided nearly 22 percent of all voluntary aid to the academy, but since 1970, their share of total voluntary support decreased 15 percent. At the same time, alumni increased their share of aid by over 11 percent and corporations increased their share by two-thirds. Religious denominations and consortia decreased their share by 39 percent, while the share of aid from friends ("non-alumni individuals") fell 2 percent. The most important decrease in aid, however, is that of foundations, for their 15 percent decline in share represents the largest revenue loss. Foundation grants from 1950 to 1986 totalled over $17 billion, nearly 73 percent more than the gifts of religious denominations and consortia, whose share also decreased noticeably. Also, the foundations' 22 percent share of aid since 1950 is nearly double the 13 percent share of religious denominations and consortia.

(Note: Chapter Two, Method of the Study, is not included in the Summary and Recommendations chapter.)

SUMMARY OF FINDINGS

Chapter Three: The History of Foundations and Higher Education

Few institutions bear the mark of philanthropy as noticeably as higher education. Hollis (1938) notes the "kinship" of foundations and higher education, while Keppel (1930) observes that the foundation's nearest relative is the university. Studies by the Council on Foundations show that foundation officers are often recruited from colleges and universities and that foundations use faculty to evaluate grant requests. Curti and Nash (1965) consider foundations to be the "telling force" in higher education, and educational philanthropists have been cited for the "magnitude of their support and the weight of their influence" (Cowley 1980). Considerable credit for the progress of American higher education therefore belongs to foundations, for they have directly or indirectly influenced "every American college and university" (Cowley 1980).

Education and particularly higher education have been favored by foundations since at least 1920. Lindeman (1936) found that from 1920 to 1930, all forms of education received 43 percent of the grants of the 100 largest foundations, and over 60 percent of the awards to education went to higher education institutions. Lindeman's 1936 discovery that over 60 percent of foundation grants went to higher education is supported by a National Planning Association study reported by Cheit and Lobman (1979) which found that 78 percent of foundation grants to education were for higher education. In the 1980s, higher education continued to receive the majority of foundation grants to education. A survey of 459 large foundations by the Foundation Center showed that from 1982 to 1985, higher education received 70 percent of foundation grants to all forms of education. In 1982, higher education received nearly 73 percent of foundation grants to education, but higher education's share of foundation grants to all forms of education declined to 68 percent in 1985.

The financial contributions of foundations to education over the past three decades include the following highlights. From 1960 to 1969, education was the leading recipient of foundation funds, garnering 31 percent of foundation grants in 1960 and 36 percent in 1969 (The Foundation Center 1971). From 1970 to 1979, education continued to be the leading recipient of foundation funds, receiving 36 percent of foundation grants in 1970, but slipping to 25 percent in 1979 (The Foundation Center, selected years). In 1980, education fell to third position among the seven fields of interest of the Foundation Center, as health acquired 25 percent of foundation grants, welfare 24 percent, and education 22 percent (The Foundation Center, selected years). In 1984, education continued to rank third among the Foundation Center's seven fields of interest, as welfare acquired 28 percent of foundation grants, health 24 percent, and education 17 percent (The Foundation Center, selected years). In 1985, education again ranked third among the Foundation Center's seven fields of interest, as welfare acquired 26 percent of foundation grants, health 24 percent, and education 17 percent (The Foundation Center, selected years).

Highlights of the programmatic contributions of foundations to higher education include:

- The definition of a college encouraged by the Carnegie Foundation for the Advancement of Teaching (Macdonald 1956; Hechinger 1967; Cowley 1980)
- Admission criteria, curriculum standards, and the "Carnegie unit" by the Carnegie Foundation for the Advancement of Teaching (Curti and Nash 1965)
- Endowment grants in 1925 of nearly $60 million by the General Education Board (*General Education Board* 1915)
- Reform of medical education by the General Education Board (*General Education Board* 1915)
- Insurance coverage and retirement annuities for faculty by the

Carnegie Foundation for the Advancement of Teaching (Pritchett 1916; Carnegie 1920)

- Research on education, natural science, social science, law, medicine, engineering, and the arts and humanities (Curti and Nash 1965; Hechinger 1967; Cowley 1980)
- Improving the accessibility of higher education to women and strengthening academic programs in women's colleges (Curti and Nash 1965)
- Expanding the accessibility of higher education to blacks and strengthening historically black colleges (*Proceedings of the Trustees of the Peabody Education Fund* 1875; Curti and Nash 1965; Hechinger 1967) and
- Instructional equipment, student aid, doctoral and post-doctoral fellowships, research on higher education, and the preservation of liberal arts colleges.

SUMMARY OF FINDINGS

Chapter Four: Dimensions of Foundations: Quantitative

Of the nation's approximately 25,000 foundations, about 5,100 hold 97 percent of the assets of all foundations and make 92 percent of all foundation grants. The assets of the 5,100 largest foundations were nearly $90 billion in 1985, while their grants were over $5 billion. In absolute terms, the assets of the nation's 5,100 largest foundations have more than doubled since 1972, but when adjusted for inflation, the increase is "virtually zero" (Rudney 1987).

Nearly three-fourths of the nation's largest foundations were established after 1950, but over the past three decades, the creation rate of foundations has decreased, a phenomenon which the Foundation Center believes may be related to increased regulation of foundations and new laws restricting the tax benefits of charitable giving. From before 1910 through 1959, 2,058 foundations with at least $1 million in assets (a criterion for inclusion in the *Foundation Directory*) were established, and the average decade increase in new foundations from 1910 through 1959 was over 105 percent. However, from 1960 through 1983, the formation rate of foundations decreased, and the creation rate over the past three decades averaged a negative 48.5 percent. The decline in the formation rate of foundations since 1960 is compounded by the termination of over 10,000 foundations from 1970 through 1982 (*America's Wealthy and the Future of Foundations*, 1987).

Since the Tax Reform Act of 1969, as amended, foundations pay
an annual excise tax on net investment income and must annually
distribute 5 percent of the market value of their assets. Foundations
are prohibited from supporting political campaigns, and other regulations restrict their ownership of businesses, their administrative expenditures, and financial dealings with their founders, trustees, or
staff.

SUMMARY OF FINDINGS

Chapter Four: Dimensions of Foundations: Accessibility

The accessibility of foundations has been an issue for over half a
century, and the poor performance of foundations in communicating
with grantseekers, Congress, and the public has been criticized by
foundation observers and officers alike. Highlights of the accessibility record of foundations include the following examples.

- In the 1920s, Keppel, first President of the Carnegie Corporation, repeatedly warned foundations of the dangers of their inaccessibility.
- Lindeman (1936) discovered 202 foundations on which he
  could acquire no information.
- Hollis (1938) found that two-thirds of foundations did not publish annual reports, and many of the reports were "so general
  and condensed" that they were "meaningless."
- Embree surveyed 505 foundations in 1949 and was unable to
  get "any information at all" from 240 (Macdonald 1956).
- In the early 1950s, Congress accused foundations of "interlock—a conspiracy to collaborate in order to subvert" (Joseph
  1986a).
- Between 1951 and 1955, Rich analyzed the Internal Revenue
  Service returns of 6,000 foundations and found so many incomplete and absent returns that she reported the problem to the
  Internal Revenue Service (Rich 1962).
- In 1956, Nason found annual reports by only seventy-seven
  foundations (1977).
- In the late 1950s, the Foundation Center encountered "stiff opposition from a great many foundations" to publishing the first
  Foundation Directory (James 1973).
- In the 1960s, during hearings preceding the Tax Reform Act of
  1969, many Congressional charges against foundations concerned their secrecy.

- The United States Treasury Department (1965) reported that many foundations "attract no public attention (and) gain no public support."
- In 1966, Nason found annual reports by only 127 foundations (1977).
- Chapper (1967) found that the Internal Revenue Service rejected one-third of foundation returns because of omissions, and in 1969, Andrews discovered that fewer than 60 percent of foundation returns were acceptably complete.
- In 1971, Magat found that 981 New York foundations placed their required annual public notice in *The New York Law Journal,* while 202 placed their notice in *The New York Times,* despite a circulation difference of 8,969 for the *Law Journal* versus 846,132 for the *Times* (James 1973).
- In 1973, only 193 foundations published annual reports, and the absentees included 79 of the 141 largest foundations (Friedman 1973).
- In 1974, the Grantmanship Center received only 759 responses (14.5 percent) from the 5,454 foundations in the *Foundation Directory* to a request for basic public information.
- In 1975, the Council on Foundations found annual reports by only 381 of the nation's approximately 27,000 foundations.
- In 1982, Crossland and Trachtenberg found annual reports by only 465 of the nation's approximately 25,000 foundations.
- In 1983, Bothwell testified before Congress that 30 percent of the nation's 208 largest foundations refused to provide information about their activities after "as many as six requests" (Magat 1983b).
- In 1985, the Foundation Center located annual reports by only 625 of the nation's approximately 25,000 foundations.

SUMMARY OF FINDINGS

Chapter Four: Dimensions of Foundations: Personnel

Perhaps the most striking characteristic of the personnel of foundations is their scarcity, for only about 1,500 of the nation's 25,000 foundations employ staff. Other personal, educational, and professional characteristics of foundation staff include the following highlights.

- Approximately 6,000 persons work in foundations, but only half hold professional posts. Moreover, two-thirds of all foundation staff are employed by only 400 foundations (Boris 1984).

- A relationship with the donor or a trustee of a foundation is a key factor in securing foundation employment (Andrews 1956; Nielsen 1972).
- Ninety-two percent of a sample of 49 foundation officers said that they were recruited for their posts through personal contacts. Only 8 percent said that they were employed through an advertisement or employment agency (Odendahl, Boris, and Daniels 1985).
- Foundation employment appears to have a certain degree of adventitiousness, for few foundation officers consciously planned for foundation service (Andrews 1956; Zurcher and Dustan 1972; Odendahl, Boris, and Daniels 1985). For example, only ten of 298 foundation officers surveyed by Zurcher and Dustan (1972) said that they had planned in any way for foundation employment. Employment as a foundation officer, therefore, is often a combination of "acquaintanceship, fitness, and accident, in varying proportions" (Odendahl, Boris, and Daniels 1985).
- Foundation professionals come from many occupations, but 37 percent served in higher education, 12 percent served in nonprofit organizations, and 12 percent served in the United States government (Zurcher and Dustan 1972).
- In 1972, Zurcher and Dustan found that only 4 percent of foundation executives had worked in another foundation, but ten years later, Boris discovered that the portion had risen to 30 percent, suggesting an influx of staff to foundations.
- Sixty-two percent of foundation professionals hold advanced degrees—32 percent with doctorates or law degrees and 30 percent with master's degrees (Boris 1982b). Odendahl, Boris, and Daniels (1985) found that more than half of foundation professionals were graduates of Ivy League colleges and universities.
- Women hold 43 percent of the professional posts in foundations (Odendahl and Boris (1983a), but only one-fourth of the chief executive officer positions (Boris 1982b). More than half of the women holding chief executive officer posts lead small foundations with less than $10 million in assets (Boris 1984).
- Minorities hold 10 percent of professional posts in foundations, but only 1 percent of chief executive officer positions (Boris 1982). Nielsen (1972) contends that many foundations are "glaring examples of institutional racism," for they lag behind the government, churches, colleges, and universities in employ-

ing minorities in executive positions. However, Nielsen (1985) reports that in the 1980s, blacks held presidencies or board chairmanships in four of the top organizations in the foundation community: the Council on Foundations; the Ford Foundation; the Rockefeller Foundation; and the Cleveland Foundation, the nation's oldest community foundation.

• In 1984, annual salaries of foundation professionals ranged from a median of $56,300 for chief executive officers in independent and operating foundations to $20,500 for office managers in community foundations (Boris 1984).

Recommended attributes of foundation staff include common sense and "absolute integrity and imagination" (Andrews 1956), administrative competence, and "humility" (Freeman 1981). Other recommended qualities are writing and speaking skill, diligence, and curiosity. However, "soundness of judgment" is the most important attribute according to foundation professionals interviewed by Odendahl, Boris, and Daniels (1985).

SUMMARY OF FINDINGS

Chapter Five: The Process and Difficulty of Grantmaking

Despite claims that giving money away is easy, philosophers, philanthropists, and foundation officers have commented extensively on the difficulty of wisely distributing charitable funds. Good grantmaking requires patience, insight, and courage, but exacts regret, worry, and disappointment (Weaver 1965, 1967; Menninger 1981). Foundation staff lament the ambiguity, subjectivity, and impersonality of grantmaking. Many foundation officers suffer depression and self-doubt (Menninger 1981), causing James (1951) to recommend that prospective foundation officers endow themselves with "no little buoyancy of spirit." Grantmaking is "wearisome and complicated," "wrought with complications," "vexing to the soul and wearing on the liver" (Macdonald 1956, Menninger 1981).

Other findings of the study on the difficulty of grantmaking include the following highlights.

• Grantmaking is more subjective than objective and is based on the assumption that judicious funding decisions are possible. According to Odendahl and Boris (1983b), there is "no precise measuring stick" to select a successful grant project.

- Foundations rarely publicly articulate the tenets they apply in grantmaking (Kennedy 1974). Their grantmaking criteria are "rarely described" and "too rarely discussed" (Odendahl and Boris 1983b), and much of foundation grantmaking is "either secret or at least not public" (Friedman 1973).
- Grantmaking may be inherently difficult because of the danger of doing more harm than good (Pritchett 1922; Todd 1930). The difficulty of grantmaking can render the act a "rote process, a lottery, a congeries of guesswork, a charade of whim" (Mayer 1972).
- Some foundations overreact to the subjectivity of grantmaking by attempting to quantify all aspects of the process. Other foundations react to applicants by adopting an attitude of detachment which borders on arrogance (Pifer 1984b).
- Foundation staff are often the targets of animosity from rejected applicants, and the tenuous relationship with grantseekers may cause fear, anxiety, isolation, aggression, and narcissism in foundation staff (Nielsen 1972; Brim 1973; Crawshaw and Bruce 1978; Odendahl, Boris, and Daniels 1985).
- The power of money may corrupt foundation officers no less than other professionals, for arrogance is a characteristic of some foundation officers who succumb to the "God complex" (Menninger 1981).
- "A genius for charity" (Thoreau (1854) is often cited as a necessary quality for foundation officers (Keppel 1930; Perkins 1965; Nason 1977).

SUMMARY OF FINDINGS

Chapter Six: The Grantmaking Principles of Foundations
Investment: The First Principle

The "very notion" of foundation grantmaking implies "purposeful giving," not merely disposing of money. Grantmaking, therefore, should be guided by a constructive purpose (Pattillo 1973). Despite claims that their grants are venture capital, most foundations are conservative, preferring established institutions whose skills or conventional programs reduce the risk of grantmaking. In 1970, the Commission on Foundations and Private Philanthropy estimated that only 3 percent of foundation grants were innovative, and in 1972, Zurcher and Dustan reported that nearly 70 percent of foundations identified the main purpose of their grants as "supportive."

Most foundation grantees, therefore, are conventional institutions such as churches, museums, local charities, colleges, and universities (Zurcher and Dustan 1972).

Although most foundation grants are conservative, foundations have supported innovative projects such as improving race relations and financing public broadcasting. "Who else," asks Nielsen (1972), "would have put up the money for *Sesame Street?*" Although some foundations are politically liberal while others are conservative, most foundations are "neither ideological nor activist (but) down the middle of the road" (Nielsen 1985). The Investment Principle may derive from the attitudes of foundation donors and trustees, many of whom have an inherent dislike for "indiscriminate charity" (Carnegie 1900; Laski 1930; Whitaker 1974). Also, the conservatism of foundations may cause them to avoid important issues when imagination and boldness are most needed. Thus, a problem for foundations which support tradition to the exclusion of innovation is the danger of becoming irrelevant (Nason 1977; Miller 1984). "Our horizons are too close," contends Miller (1984); "our vision too dim. . . . " As problems become more complex, foundations appear impelled to "play it safer and safer" (Miller 1984).

Competence: The Second Principle

If foundation grantmaking is an investment, foundations must evaluate several characteristics of grantseekers, the most important of which is their competence. The "most ancient and useful rule" of foundations, according to Gardner, is to "find the good men and back them" (Whitaker 1974). Other questions asked by foundations of projects proposed for grants are: "Is the problem one that needs solution? Is the proposal soundly conceived to accomplish its stated objective? Is this trip really necessary?" (Mayer 1972). Townsend (1974) learned that 100 public and private grantors rated grantee competence from "very much" to "absolutely important" in grant decisions, and Mayer (1972) reports that the most important question a foundation asks when evaluating a grantseeker is: "What is the track record of the institution?"

Foundation money is rarely awarded for an idea, but rather, is given to a person with the skill and drive to fulfill an idea (Josephs 1945). Therefore, the essence of foundation grantmaking may be a "bet on an individual" (Freeman 1981). The notion that money can create ideas and that more money can create better ideas is a fallacy, according to Fosdick (1965), for without competent grantees, "money will purchase nothing but motion and futility. Money is enabling," contends Kimball (1974), "but only men produce."

Realism: The Third Principle

The realism of projects and their proposers is an essential element in foundation grantmaking. Applicants must satisfy the program interests of foundations, while demonstrating that proposed projects are feasible. The goals of many grant programs are considered to be unrealistically high by foundations, who therefore often discount proposed goals in favor of "reasonable results" (Townsend 1974). Budgets of grant proposals are carefully examined by foundations to reveal excesses or deficits in anticipated income and expenditures (Odendahl and Boris 1983b). The review of budgets also reveals the thoroughness and efficiency of applicants.

The scope of grant requests may be bounded only by the imagination of grantseekers. Foundations have received proposals to invent perpetual motion machines; melt the polar ice caps; irrigate the Sahara, the Sinai Peninsula, and Death Valley; promote "singing among boys" at naval training stations; and "harvest the ideas and constructive thoughts of the American people" (Harrison and Andrews 1946; Andrews 1956; Goulden 1971). The unrealistic nature of many grant proposals requires foundations to separate the carefully conceived applications from the "superficial, the poorly planned, and inconsequential" (Pattillo 1965).

Clarity: The Fourth Principle

The clarity of a grant proposal is a "critical factor, if not *the* critical factor" in obtaining a grant (Lefferts 1982). Although foundation officers encourage applicants to use simple English in their proposals, many grantseekers use a language of exaggeration which I call Proposalese. Proposalese prefers the complex to the simple, the obscure to the familiar, and the long to the short.

Proposalese has three precursors: Educationese, the expression of educators; Redundancese, a language of unnecessary repetition; e.g., "free gifts," "the spread of nuclear proliferation;" and "Foundationese" (Macdonald 1956), the language of foundations, a dead language, written rather than spoken, and designed for ceremony, not utility.

The first characteristic of Proposalese is its interchangeability; three examples of Proposalese, "intellectual continuum," "perceptual parameter," and "developmental linkage," can easily become "perceptual continuum," "developmental parameter," "intellectual linkage," "developmental continuum," "perceptual linkage," or "intellectual parameter." McGuire (1981), who read some 5,000 grant proposals while working at a large foundation, noticed a "universal proposal language" so similar that entire paragraphs could be switched from proposal to proposal. The second characteristic of Proposalese is that it is purposely unclear. The authors of a study on foreign students in American colleges worried that their report was not "perspicuous." The authors feared that their study was not clear, but did they use the word, clear? No, they used perspicuous, an unclear word for clear. The third characteristic of Proposalese is its self-indulgence; in Proposalese, all ideas are "unique," all programs are "excellent," and all results are "outstanding." Fund raisers do not merely raise money; they are "development officers" who turn "germinal but viable concepts" into "seminal opportunities" to "maximize the mileage" of "seed capital" so that grants will have a "multiplier effect" and "make the peaks higher" (Whitaker 1974).

Clear grant proposals are essential, for if an applicant cannot clearly state its case, how will it be able to carry out a project? If the intent of a proposal is not clearly explained, the idea behind the proposal probably is not clear either. Says Dunham of the Carnegie Corporation: "If people can't write in English," the proposal is "probably not worth funding" (Perry 1982).

Continuity: The Fifth Principle

The continuity of grant programs is important to foundations because they are reluctant to become the sole or even the major source of an organization's support (Whitaker 1974). Many foundations believe that grantees should not rely on foundations for "continuity and stability" (Weaver 1967). Therefore, foundations closely examine the projects for their potential self-sufficiency, noting that grantseekers often claim that programs will be independent by the expiration of grants. Such predictions, however, are seldom realistic (Mayer 1972). Indeed, Goulden (1971) believes that many grantees could not become self-sufficient "unless they robbed banks."

Because of the importance of the continuity of grant programs, foundations are reducing the duration of grants or awarding multi-year grants whose amounts decrease in their latter years. Foundations recognize that their grants may cause agencies to grow much faster than their normal rate of development and that grants can cause "organizational cancer" (Macdonald 1956). Thibault (1973) studied the effects of grant programs in universities, and he warns that dependence on grants can be detrimental to institutional autonomy. Despite their efforts to reduce commitments to grantees, foundations have found few easy ways to withdraw from projects which they have supported for years. Hollis (1938) believes that foundations should carefully evaluate the willingness of grantseekers to continue programs after grants expire. He also contends that institutions should pursue grants only when they are fully committed to their continuance. "Many a long journey begins with a single step," writes Kimball (1974). "But many a long journey is never completed because the steps fail to continue."

Trust: The Sixth Principle

Trust between grantor and grantee is a factor on which the other five grantmaking principles depend. The relationship of foundation and grantseeker is subtle and sensitive, for the requirements of a foundation must be balanced with the autonomy of a grantee (Hertz and Kurzig 1983). The Council on Foundations (1980 and 1984) has encouraged foundations and applicants to recognize their "community of interest" and to develop a relationship of "mutual respect, candor, and understanding." Miller (1984) believes that foundations and grantseekers are "interdependent," and Joseph (1986d) contends that both parties have a responsibility to "feel more directly the emotional effects of the transaction."

However, the relationship of grantor and grantee is often like that of a "banker and a borrower" (Joseph 1986d), for a "human connection is not likely to be made" (Joseph 1986e). The relationship of foundations and grantseekers is also often manipulative, for both parties have been guilty of deception, rudeness, and aggression (Menninger 1981). Foundations violate the principle of trust when they are arrogant or less than open when discussing the reasons for rejected proposals. Although grantseekers may not participate directly in the grantmaking process, they are not passive onlookers (Magat 1983a). Grantseekers violate the principle of trust when they are hypocritical, offensive, or overly aggressive or when they wheedle, cajole, or threaten foundations (Menninger 1981). One of the greatest evils in grantmaking, therefore, is "resistance to intimacy" (Crawshaw and Bruce 1978), which is the failure of grantors and grantees to trust each other, resorting instead to a "massive confidence game (of) terrible tricks" (Johnson 1975b).

RECOMMENDATIONS

The Study of Philanthropy

The study of philanthropy is relatively new, and foundations should be at its forefront by encouraging research on philanthropy in universities. The first mission of the centers should be to enrich the literature on foundations, for there are too few scholarly works on foundations. Major foundations should establish publishing departments following the lead of the Russell Sage Foundation which has published works on philanthropy. The literature on foundations requires expansion, and a model for foundations to follow would be the effort of the Carnegie Council on Policy Studies in Higher Education to enrich the higher education literature in the 1970s.

Permanent Commission on Foundations

The last major study of foundations, excluding works by individual authors, was in 1975 by the Commission on Private Philanthropy and Public Needs. Another major report on foundations is needed, and a commission should produce a major study of foundations every decade.

Renew the Partnership of Foundations and Higher Education

Foundations have been instrumental in the development of higher education, and they should continue, rather than decrease, their commitment to the academy. Foundations need to consider higher education as more than merely a "service provider" (Marchese, Bernstein, and Newman 1985), and their commitment to the academy should be distinct, rather than as a part of "science, technology, and the economy" (Sleeper 1985).

If foundations need to know higher education as more than another service provider, higher education needs to know a great deal more about foundations. College development officers, especially, should improve their understanding of foundations beyond data in the *Foundation Directory* and other sourcebooks for grants. The literature on foundations may require expansion, but the familiarity of many higher education officers with foundations may extend no further than the latest guidebook on acquiring grants.

The Accessibility of Foundations

The Foundation Center should continue its noteworthy effort in publishing the *Foundation Directory* and in developing collections on foundations in regional libraries. Foundations, rather than resisting publication in the *Directory,* should cooperate. The Center should consider developing an abbreviated *Directory* questionnaire similar to the Internal Revenue Service 1040 EZ Form for foundations with limited grants or staff. A "Short Form" questionnaire may help small foundations list information in the *Directory,* while dispelling the contention of some foundations that a complicated questionnaire impedes participation. The Foundation Center should also relax its criteria for including foundations in the *Directory.* Currently, inclusion is generally limited to foundations with assets of at least $1 million and annual grants at least $100,000. The criteria on assets and grants should be changed to $500,000 and $50,000, respectively.

Directories of Foundations

More agencies of state and local governments should produce directories of foundations, and lists of foundations maintained by Departments of State or Community Affairs in state governments should be more widely circulated. Human service directories of local governments, health and welfare councils, and regional planning commissions should include foundations.

United States Congress

The accessibility of foundations has been and continues to be a major Congressional concern (Joseph 1983e). A report on the accessibility of foundations should be prepared yearly for Congress by the Treasury Department or the General Accounting Office, and national lawmakers should keep the accessibility issue on their agenda until the problem is solved.

Council on Foundations

In addition to publishing policy statements encouraging foundations to be more accessible (1973b, 1980, 1984a), the Council on Foundations should update its book, *Public Information Handbook for Foundations* (Richman 1973). Also, the Council on Foundations should sponsor workshops for foundations on communication practices.

Annual Public Notice

The legislation requiring foundations to advertise in one newspaper that their Internal Revenue Service return is available for public inspection should be changed. Local foundations should be required to place the notice in the newspaper with the largest circulation in their community. Regional foundations should be required to place the notice in the three largest newspapers in their service area. National foundations should be required to place the notice in the seven largest newspapers in the United States.

Foundation Annual Reports

Every foundation, regardless of the size of its assets, grants, or staff, should publish an annual report. The publication should list program interests, grants and grantees, assets, trustees, executive staff, proposal guidelines, and a description of the proposal review process. Without exception, the report should contain the address and telephone number of the foundation. For small foundations, a folder or one-page report may suffice. The Council on Foundations, the Foundation Center, and the United States Congress should continue to urge all foundations to issue annual reports.

Foundations should also publish semi-annual newsletters on grants and program interests. Foundations should conduct public forums to explain their grantmaking interests, meet the donee group, and assess community needs. Groups of local or regional foundations could co-sponsor such forums.

Communication Staff in Foundations

Foundations should employ a public relations officer, retain communications consultants, or enlist the aid of institutions such as colleges that have communications personnel. The claim by some foundations that limited assets preclude hiring communications staff is no justification for poor accessibility.

Increased Diversity of Foundation Trustees

Studies of the characteristics of foundation trustees show that most trustees are mature, white males from business, law, and finance. Also, many trustees have a personal or professional relationship with the donor of the foundation, the donor's family, or the donor's corporation.

Foundations should voluntarily broaden the diversity of their boards, and Congress, the Foundation Center, and the Council on Foundations should continue to urge diversity in trustees. Foundations should enlist the aid of the Association of Governing Boards to broaden trustee representation and strengthen governance. Although foundation boards are becoming more diverse, the proportion of women and blacks, estimated at 25 and 5 percent, respectively, is still too low. Moreover, representation of members of the donee group on foundation boards is rare. The most common characteristics of foundation trustees should be diversity and wisdom, rather than a relationship with the foundation donor.

Increased Numbers of Foundation Staff

Scarcity is the dominant feature of foundation staff, for only about 7 percent of the nation's foundations employ professional staff. Nearly every foundation should employ full or part-time staff. Small foundations should either retain a consultant or pool resources with other foundations to employ at least one staff member. More women and blacks should be admitted to foundation posts. Staff vacancies in foundations should be advertised in such publications as *Foundation News* and *The Chronicle of Higher Education*. Bankers, lawyers, or employees of the donor's corporation who serve as part-time foundation staff should improve their understanding of grantmaking.

*   *

Despite their notable contributions to education, science, social service, and the arts and humanities, foundations are among the nation's least understood institutions. The inadequate understanding of foundations by higher education officials underscores the scope of the problem, for higher education has had a closer relationship with foundations than perhaps any other sector.

Renewing the partnership of foundations and higher education is not the responsibility solely of foundations, for the relationship can be strengthened only by both parties. The first step in the process, however, belongs to higher education, for the academy's poor understanding of foundations will impede any effort to strengthen the partnership. Higher education's first task, therefore, is to increase its knowledge of the people and practices of foundations.

*   *   *

BIBLIOGRAPHY

Allen, Yorke. "How Foundations Evaluate Requests." In *Foundations: Twenty Viewpoints*, edited by F. Emerson Andrews. New York: Russell Sage Foundation, 1965.

Allen, William H. *Rockefeller: Giant, Dwarf, Symbol*. New York: Institute for Public Service, 1930.

American Association of Fund Raising Counsel. *Giving USA*. New York: 1980–1985.

American Association of University Professors. "Weighted Average Salaries and Average Compensation." *AAUP Bulletin*, June 2, 1970.

American Council on Education. *1984–85 Fact Book on Higher Education*. Washington: 1984.

Anderson, Charles J. *Conditions Affecting College and University Financial Strength*. Washington: American Council on Education, 1985.

Andres, Richard H. *Foundation Relations Manual*. Washington: American College Relations Association, 1962.

Andrews, F. Emerson. *Philanthropic Giving*. New York: Russell Sage Foundation, 1950.

Andrews, F. Emerson. *Corporation Giving*. New York: Russell Sage Foundation, 1952.

Andrews, F. Emerson. *Attitudes Toward Giving*. New York: Russell Sage Foundation, 1953.

Andrews, F. Emerson. Preface to *Operating Principles of the Larger Foundations*, by Joseph Kiger. New York: Russell Sage Foundation, 1954.

Andrews, F. Emerson. *Philanthropic Foundations*. New York: Russell Sage Foundation, 1956.

Andrews, F. Emerson, ed. *Foundations: Twenty Viewpoints*. New York: Russell Sage Foundation, 1965.

Andrews, F. Emerson. *Patman and Foundations: Review and Assessment*. New York: The Foundation Center, 1968.

Andrews, F. Emerson. *Philanthropy in the United States*. New York: The Foundation Center, 1974.

Archabal, John. "Inspecting the Damage." *Foundation News*, March/April 1984.

Armbruster, Timothy. "Foundation Policy Review." *The Philanthropy Monthly*, April 1980.

Ary, Donald, Lucy Chester Jacobs, and Asghar Razavieh. *Introduction to Research in Education*. New York: Holt, Rinehart, and Winston, 1972.

Auchincloss, Louis. "Ah, What Would Veblen Say?" *Forbes*, October 1, 1984.

161

Bailey, Anne Lowrey. "So You Want to Get a Grant." *Change,* January/ February 1985.

Bailey, Anne Lowrey. "With 3,200 Grants a Year, Alcoa's Director of Corporate Giving Is Learning How to Say No." *The Chronicle of Higher Education,* September 16, 1987.

Bailey, Anne Lowrey. "Corporations Starting to Make Grants to Public Schools, Diverting Some Funds Once Earmarked for Colleges." *The Chronicle of Higher Education,* February 10, 1988.

Barron, Deborah. "Setting Priorities for the 80s." *Foundation News,* November/December 1980.

Barzun, Jacques. *Teacher in America.* Boston: Little, Brown, 1944.

Barzun, Jacques. *The House of Intellect.* New York: Harper and Row, 1959.

Barzun, Jacques and Henry F. Graff. *The Modern Researcher.* New York: Harcourt, Brace, and World, 1970.

Behar, Richard. "They Gave Too Much." *Forbes,* October 1, 1984.

Berelson, Bernard. *Content Analysis in Communication Research.* New York: Free Press, 1952.

Berelson, Bernard. "Content Analysis." In *Handbook of Social Psychology,* edited by G. Lindzey. Reading, Massachusetts: Addison-Wesley, 1954.

Best, John. *Research in Education.* Englewood Cliffs, New Jersey: Prentice-Hall, 1970.

Bolling, Landrum. "What Every Trust Officer Should Know about Philanthropy and Foundations." *Trusts and Estates,* December 1978.

Bonine, Robert. "One Part Science, One Part Art." *Foundation News,* November/December 1971.

Boorstin, Daniel. *The Decline of Radicalism.* New York: Random House, 1963.

Boris, Elizabeth, Patricia Unkle, and Carol Hooper. "Tax and Expenditure Limitations." *Foundation News,* May/June 1980.

Boris, Elizabeth and Patricia Unkle. "Council Survey Highlights Foundation Staffing." *Foundation News,* May/June 1980.

Boris, Elizabeth. "Trustees and CEOs." *Foundation News,* January/February 1982a.

Boris, Elizabeth. "Survey of 1982 Compensation and Benefits Finds More Women Foundation Executives." *Foundation News,* November/December 1982b.

Boris, Elizabeth and Carol Hooper. "Highlights of Council's Compensation and Benefits Survey." *Foundation News,* November/December 1982.

Boris, Elizabeth. "What We Have Learned." *Foundation News,* July/August 1984.

Boris, Elizabeth. "Increasing What We Know." *Foundation News,* May/June 1985.

Boris, Elizabeth. "New Studies Give Definition to Third Sector." *Foundation News,* May/June 1986.

Bothwell, Robert. Testimony before the Sub-Committee on Commerce, Consumer, and Monetary Affairs. Washington: House of Representatives, May 11, 1983.

Bowen, Howard R. *The Costs of Higher Education*. San Francisco: Jossey-Bass, 1980.

Bradley, William. "Share, But Not in Writing." *Foundation News*, July/August 1983.

Branch, Taylor. "The Case Against Foundations." *Washington Monthly*, July 1971.

Brecht, Charles. *Foundation Relations Manual*. Washington: American College Public Relations Association, 1962.

Bremmer, Robert H. *American Philanthropy*. University of Chicago Press, 1960.

Brim, Orville. "Do We Know What We Are Doing?" In *The Future of Foundations*, edited by Fritz Heimann. Englewood Cliffs, New Jersey: Prentice-Hall, 1973.

Broce, Thomas. *Fund Raising*. University of Oklahoma Press, 1979.

Broce, Thomas. "New Directions for Foundations in the 1980s." In *New Directions for Institutional Advancement*, edited by J. David Ross. San Francisco: Jossey-Bass, November 1981.

Broughton, Philip S. "The Economic Function of Foundations." In *Foundations: Twenty Viewpoints*, edited by F. Emerson Andrews. New York: Russell Sage Foundation, 1965.

Brown, Dyke. "Ford and Other Foundations in Public Affairs." In *Foundations: Twenty Viewpoints*, edited by F. Emerson Andrews. New York: Russell Sage Foundation, 1965.

Brubacher, John S. and Willis Rudy. *Higher Education in Transition*. New York: Harper and Row, 1958.

Bundy, McGeorge. *Foundation Trustees: Their Moral and Social Responsibilities*. New York: The Ford Foundation, 1974.

Butler, Nicholas Murray. "To the National Council on Education." *Journal of Proceedings and Addresses, 1892*. New York: National Education Association, 1893.

Calhoun, Susan. "About the News." *Foundation News*, November/December 1987.

Calhoun, Susan. "About the News." *Foundation News*, January/February 1988.

Campbell, Stewart F. "The Impact on Foundations of the Tax Reform Act of 1969." In *New Directions for Institutional Advancement*, edited by J. David Ross. San Francisco: Jossey-Bass, 1981.

Candler, Warren Akin. *Dangerous Donations and Degrading Doles*. Atlanta: Lester Book Company, 1909.

Cannon, Cornelia J. "Philanthropic Doubts." *Atlantic Monthly*, September 1921.

Caplin, Mortimer M. "Foundations and the Government: Some Observations on the Future." In *Foundations: Twenty Viewpoints*, edited by F. Emerson Andrews. New York: Russell Sage Foundation, 1965.

Carey, Sarah C. "Philanthropy and the Powerless." In *Private Giving and Public Policy*. New York: Commission on Private Philanthropy and Public Needs, 1975.

Carnegie, Andrew. "Wealth." *North American Review*, 1889.

Carnegie, Andrew. *The Gospel of Wealth and Other Timely Essays.* New York: The Century Company, 1900.

Carnegie, Andrew. Letter to *The Independent,* 1913.

Carnegie, Andrew. *Autobiography of Andrew Carnegie.* Boston: 1920.

Carnegie Corporation. *Annual Report.* New York: 1955.

Carnegie Council on Policy Studies on Higher Education. *Three Thousand Futures.* San Francisco: Jossey-Bass, 1980.

Case, Everett. "Philanthropy as a Social Investment." In *Foundations: Twenty Viewpoints,* edited by F. Emerson Andrews. New York: Russell Sage Foundation, 1965.

Cattell, J. McKeen. *Carnegie Pensions.* New York: Science Press, 1919.

Chapper, Frank M. "Disclosure and Reporting: Present Requirements and Forms." In *Proceedings of the Eighth Biennial Conference on Charitable Foundations.* New York: Bender, 1967.

Cheit, Earl F. *The New Depression in Higher Education.* New York: McGraw-Hill, 1971.

Cheit, Earl F. *The New Depression in Higher Education—Two Years Later.* New York: McGraw-Hill, 1973.

Cheit, Earl F. and Theodore Lobman. *Private Philanthropy and Higher Education.* Washington: Commission on Private Philanthropy and Public Needs, 1977.

Cheit, Earl F. and Theodore Lobman. *Foundations and Higher Education.* San Francisco: Jossey-Bass, 1979.

Chronicle of Higher Education. "Number of Foundations and Value of Their Assets Surged in the 1980's, New Compilation Finds." November 18, 1987.

Cleveland Foundation. *Staff Reference Manual.* 1973.

Coffman, Harold. *American Foundations.* New York: Association Press, 1932.

Colwell, Mary Anna. "Philanthropic Foundations and Public Policy." Ph.D. dissertation, University of California, 1980.

Commission on Foundations and Private Philanthropy. *Private Giving and Public Policy.* University of Chicago Press, 1970.

Commission on Private Philanthropy and Public Needs. *Giving in America.* Washington: 1975.

Community Renewal Society. *Chicago Reporter.* July 1973.

Coolbrith, Alison G. "Healthy Self-Analysis Strengthens the Field." *Foundation News,* July/August 1985.

Corbally, John E. "In the Money." *Currents,* July/August 1984.

Council for Financial Aid to Education. *Voluntary Support of Education: 1982–83.* New York: 1984.

Council for Financial Aid to Education. *Voluntary Support of Education: 1983–84.* New York: 1985.

Council for Financial Aid to Education. *Voluntary Support of Education: 1984–85.* New York: 1986.

Council for Financial Aid to Education. *Voluntary Support of Education: 1985–86.* New York: 1987.

Council for the Advancement and Support of Education. "Cultivating Foundations." *Currents,* July/August 1984.

Council on Foundations. "A Policy on Public Information." *Foundation News*, January/February 1973a.

Council on Foundations. *Some General Principles and Guidelines for Grant-Making Foundations*. New York: 1973b.

Council on Foundations. *Recommended Principles and Practices for Effective Grantmaking*. New York: 1980.

Council on Foundations. "Highlights of the Council's Legislation and Regulation Survey." *Foundation News*, July/August 1981.

Council on Foundations. *Principles and Practices for Effective Grantmaking*. New York: 1984a.

Council on Foundations. *The Grantmaking Process*. New York: 1984b.

Cowley, W. H. *Presidents, Professors and Trustees*. San Francisco: Jossey-Bass, 1980.

Crawshaw, R. and J. Bruce. "Reflections on the Art of Giving." *Foundation News*, January/February 1978.

Crossland, Fred and Stephen Trachtenberg. "Fifteen Pleas to Fund Raisers and Foundations." *Educational Record*, Summer 1982.

Cunninggim, Merrimon. *Private Money and Public Service*. New York: McGraw-Hill, 1972.

Curti, Merle. "American Philanthropy and the National Character." *American Quarterly*, Winter 1958.

Curti, Merle and Roderick Nash. *Philanthropy in the Shaping of American Higher Education*. New Brunswick, New Jersey: Rutgers University Press, 1965.

Dane, J. "Analysis of the Trends of Financial Support of Philanthropic Foundations to General Programs in Higher Education." Ph.D. dissertation, University of Pittsburgh, 1974.

Dayton, Kenneth N. "Identifying Responsibilities for CEOs, Chairs, and Trustees." *Foundation News*, May/June 1985.

DeBakey, Lois. "The Persuasive Proposal." *Foundation News*, July/August 1977.

DeTocqueville, Alexis. *Democracy in America*. New York: Alfred Knopf, 1945.

Desruisseaux, Paul. "Foundations Seek Better Relations on Capitol Hill." *The Chronicle of Higher Education*, January 30, 1985a.

Desruisseaux, Paul. "Notes on Philanthropy." *The Chronicle of Higher Education*, March 13, 1985b.

Desruisseaux, Paul. "Study Finds Slowdown in Formation of New Foundations." *The Chronicle of Higher Education*, May 8, 1985c.

Desruisseaux, Paul. "New Agenda: Public Policy on Schools and Colleges." *The Chronicle of Higher Education*, August 7, 1985d.

Desruisseaux, Paul. "What Would Andrew Carnegie Think . . . Today?" *The Chronicle of Higher Education*, August 7, 1985e.

Desruisseaux, Paul. "Notes on Foundations." *The Chronicle of Higher Education*, December 11, 1985f.

Desruisseaux, Paul. "Reporting to the Public: Some Foundations Do, Most Don't." *The Chronicle of Higher Education*, January 22, 1986a.

Desruisseaux, Paul. "Foundations Are Asked to Help Train and Encourage New Leaders." *The Chronicle of Higher Education*, April 30, 1986b.

Desruisseaux, Paul. "A Foundation Head Puts His Faith in Higher Education." *The Chronicle of Higher Education*, September 3, 1986c.

Desruisseaux, Paul. "Ford Foundation, Flush with Recent Earnings, Rethinks." *The Chronicle of Higher Education*, September 3, 1986d.

Desruisseaux, Paul. "30-Year-Old Foundation Center Keeps Track of Where the Money Goes." *The Chronicle of Higher Education*, October 8, 1986e.

Desruisseaux, Paul. "Aging of 'Baby Boomers' Seen Likely to Affect Corporate Giving." *The Chronicle of Higher Education*, April 8, 1987a.

Desruisseaux, Paul. "Health of Foundation Philanthropy Assessed in New Study of Giving by Rich Americans." *The Chronicle of Higher Education*, May 6, 1987b.

Desruisseaux, Paul. "Conservative Foundations to Turn Attention to Philanthropy Itself." *The Chronicle of Higher Education*, September 2, 1987c.

Dickinson, Joseph. "A Long-Time Grant Seeker to Foundations: Let's Discuss Goals." *Foundation News*, July/August 1973.

Dodge, Faith Hunter. "In the Service of Humanity." *Pan-American*, December 1928.

Donee Group. *Private Philanthropy: Report and Recommendations.* 1976.

Edie, John. "Influencing Public Policy: The Legal Limits." *Foundation News*, March/April 1985a.

Edie, John. "Chances Are Your IRS 990-PF Tax Form Is Incomplete." *Foundation News*, July/August 1985b.

Eisenberg, Pablo. "Philanthropic Ethics from a Donee Perspective." *Foundation News*, September/October 1983.

Eliot, T. S. *The Complete Poems and Plays.* Harcourt, Brace, and World, 1952.

Elliott, Eleanor. "On Being a Trustee." *Foundation News,* May/June 1984.

Ellison, Jerome. "Who Gets Your Charity Dollars?" *Saturday Evening Post,* June 16, 1954.

Embree, Edwin. "The Business of Giving Away Money." *Harper's Monthly,* August 1930.

Embree, Edwin. "Timid Billions: Are The Foundations Doing Their Job?" *Harper's,* March 1949.

Esposito, Virginia. "Serving Better by Cooperating More." *Foundation News,* July/August 1983.

Evans, Eli N. "Creativity as the Cornerstone of Philanthropy." *Foundation News,* May/June 1983.

Faust, Clarence H. "The Role of the Foundation in Education: Two Opportunities." *Saturday Review,* 1952.

Feldman, Kenneth and Theodore Newcomb. *The Impact of College on Students.* San Francisco: Jossey-Bass, 1969.

Feldman, Kenneth. "Using the Work of Others: Some Observations on Reviewing and Integrating." *Sociology of Education,* Winter 1971.

Ferguson, Esther B. "Who's in Charge of Corporate Giving?" *The New York Times,* June 30, 1985.

Finkelstein, Martin J. "Three Decades of Research on American Academics." Ph.D. dissertation, State University of New York at Buffalo, 1978.

Finkelstein, Martin J. *The American Academic Profession*. Ohio State University Press, 1984.

Finn, Chester E. *Scholars, Dollars, and Bureaucrats*. Washington: Brookings Institution, 1978.

Finn, Chester E. "Educational Excellence: Eight Elements." *Foundation News*, March/April 1986.

Fisher, James, ed. *Presidential Leadership in Advancement Activities*. San Francisco: Jossey-Bass, 1980.

Flexner, Abraham. *Medical Education in the United States and Canada*. New York: Carnegie Foundation for the Advancement of Teaching, 1910.

Flexner, Abraham. "Private Fortunes and the Public Future." *Atlantic Monthly*, August 1935.

Flexner, Abraham. *Funds and Foundations*. New York: Harper and Brothers, 1952.

Foote, Joseph. "Stretching the Career Ladder." *Foundation News*, January/February 1985.

Foote, Joseph. "For RAGs It's Riches." *Foundation News*, July/August 1986a.

Foote, Joseph. "No, They're NOT Foundations." *Foundation News*, September/October 1986b.

Fosdick, Raymond B. *The Story of the Rockefeller Foundation: 1913 to 1950*. New York: Harper and Brothers, 1952.

Fosdick, Raymond B. "The Usefulness of Money." In *Foundations: Twenty Viewpoints*, edited by F. Emerson Andrews. New York: Russell Sage Foundation, 1965.

Foundation Center. *Annual Report*. New York: 1964.

Foundation Center. *Foundation Directory*. New York: Columbia University Press, 1971.

Foundation Center. *Foundation Directory*. New York: Columbia University Press, 1985.

Fox, Thomas H. "Persistent Criticisms." *Foundation News*, November/December 1987.

Freeman, David F. "Personality Traits of Small Foundations." *Foundation News*, September/October 1980.

Freeman, David F. *The Handbook on Private Foundations*. New York: Council on Foundations, 1981.

Fremont-Smith, Marion R. *Foundations and Government*. New York: Russell Sage Foundation, 1965.

Freud, Anna. *The Ego and the Mechanism of Defence*. London: Hogarth Press, 1948.

Friedman, Richard E. "Private Foundation-Government Relationships." In *The Future of Foundations*, edited by Fritz Heimann. Englewood Cliffs, New Jersey, Prentice-Hall, 1973.

General Education Board. *The General Education Board: An Account of Its Activities, 1902–1914*. New York: 1915.

General Education Board. *Annual Report, 1925–1926*. New York: 1926.

Getzels, Jacob. "Problem-Finding and Research in Educational Administration." In *Educational Administration as a Social Process*. New York: Harper and Row, 1968.

Glass, Gene. "Primary, Secondary, and Meta-Analysis of Research." *Educational Researcher*, November 1976.

Glass, Gene, Barry McGaw, and Mary Lee Smith. *Meta-Analysis in Social Research*. Beverly Hills, California: Sage Publications, 1981.

Goheen, Robert F. "On Foundations: Some Outgoing Observations." New York: Council on Foundations, 1977.

Gomberg, Irene L. and Frank J. Atelsek. *Trends in Financial Indicators of Colleges and Universities*. Washington: American Council on Education, 1981.

Goodwin, William M. "Thirty Financial Questions to Cut Funding Risks." *Foundation News*, March/April 1976.

Gorman, Jim. "A Congressional Call for More Accountability." *Foundation News*, May/June 1983a.

Gorman, Jim. "Traversing the Spectrum." *Foundation News*, July/August 1983b.

Gorman, Jim. "Differences of Opinion." *Foundation News*, July/August 1985.

Gottlieb, Leslie. "Reaching the Media." *Foundation News*, January/February 1986.

Goulden, Joseph. *The Money Givers*. New York: Random House, 1971.

Goulden, Joseph. "If I Were Head of a Foundation." *Foundation News*, July/August 1972.

Greenleaf, Robert K. "The Trustee: The Buck Starts Here." *Foundation News*, July/August 1973.

Greenleaf, Robert K. *Trustees as Servants*. Cambridge, Massachusetts: Center for Applied Studies, 1974a.

Greenleaf, Robert K. "Prudence and Creativity: A Trustee Responsibility." *Foundation News*, May/June 1974b.

Gregg, Alan. "Notes on Giving." 1953.

Guba, Egon G. *Toward a Methodology of Naturalistic Inquiry in Education Evaluation*. Los Angeles: University of California, Center for the Study of Evaluation, 1978.

Hahn, Maxwell. "The American Foundations Face the Future." Paper presented at a meeting of the American Association of Fund Raising Counsel, New York, February 1957.

Hallahan, Kathleen. "The Great Numbers Debate—and Why It's Important." *Foundation News*, July/August 1983.

Hallahan, Kathleen. "Big Government, Little Philanthropy." *Foundation News*, March/April 1985.

Hamburg, David. "President's Message." *Annual Report of the Carnegie Corporation*. New York: 1983.

Harrison, S. M. and F. Emerson Andrews. *American Foundations for Social Welfare*. New York, Russell Sage Foundation, 1946.

Hechinger, Fred. "The Foundations and Education." In *U.S. Philanthropic Foundations*, edited by Warren Weaver. New York: Harper and Row, 1967.

Heimann, Fritz. "Developing a Contemporary Rationale for Foundations." *Foundation News*, January/February 1972.

Heimann, Fritz, ed. *The Future of Foundations.* Englewood Cliffs, New Jersey: Prentice-Hall, 1973.

Hendrick, B. *The Life of Andrew Carnegie.* New York: Doubleday, Doran, and Company, 1932.

Hennessey, Jean L. "The Unpersuasive Proposal." *Foundation News,* July/August 1977.

Henry, William A. "An Open and Shut Case," *Foundation News,* March/April 1987.

Hertz, William and Carol Kurzig. "A Grant for Every Purpose." *Foundation News,* January/February 1983.

Hewitt, Patricia. "Arrogance Could Disrupt Work." *Foundation News,* January/February 1984.

Heymann, Richard. "The Art of Getting." *Daily Record,* October 25, 1981a.

Heymann, Richard. "The Art of Giving." *Daily Record,* October 25, 1981b.

Higgins, Robert F. "How One Foundation Developed and Implemented a New Strategy." *Foundation News,* November/December 1976.

Hirschfield, Ira S. "Foundation Work: The Who's and How's." *Foundation News,* November/December 1984.

Hodgkinson, Virginia. "Slowdown in the Sector." *Foundation News,* September/October 1986.

Hollis, Ernest. *Philanthropic Foundations and Higher Education.* New York: Columbia University Press, 1938.

Hollis, Ernest. "Evolution of the Philanthropic Foundation." *Educational Record,* October 1939.

Hollis, Ernest. "The Foundations and the Universities." *Journal of Higher Education,* November 1940.

Horowitz, David and David Kolodney. "The Foundation: Charity Begins at Home." *Ramparts,* April 1969.

House, Ernest R. *The Logic of Evaluative Argument.* Los Angeles, University of California, Center for the Study of Evaluation, 1977.

Hunter, David R. "Defining Priorities in the Public Interest." *Foundation News,* September/October 1978.

Jackson, Gregory. "Methods for Integrative Reviews." *Review of Educational Research,* Fall 1980.

Jacquette, F. Lee and Barbara. "What Makes a Good Proposal?" *Foundation News,* January/February 1973.

James, H. Thomas. "Perspectives on Internal Functioning of Foundations." In *The Future of Foundations,* edited by Fritz Heimann. Englewood Cliffs, New Jersey: Prentice-Hall, 1973.

James, Henry. "President of the Carnegie Corporation." *Appreciations of Frederick Paul Keppel.* New York: Columbia University Press, 1951.

Jellema, William. "The Red and the Black." *Liberal Education,* May 1971.

Johnson, Richard. "Writing Grant Proposals." Paper presented at the annual meeting of the Council for the Advancement and Support of Education, New York, January 1985.

Johnson, Robert M. "The Family Board—Speculating with a Point of View." *Foundation News,* January/February 1974.

Johnson, Robert M. "Notice." *Foundation News,* January/February 1975a.

Johnson, Robert M. "Where Hustle Ends and Trust Begins." *Foundation News*, May/June 1975b.

Johnson, Robert M. "Foundation Lib is Here!" *Foundation News*, September/October 1975c.

Johnson, Robert M. "We Turned You Down Because . . . " *Foundation News*, November/December 1975d.

Johnson, Robert M. "Four Parting Pearls of Wisdom and Truth." *Foundation News*, March/April 1976.

Joseph, James A. "The Donee as a Philanthropic Stakeholder." *Foundation News*, November/December 1982.

Joseph, James A. "Accountability: More Relevant Than Ever." *Foundation News*, January/February 1983a.

Joseph, James A. "Philanthropy and Politics: The 1983 Hearings." *Foundation News*, March/April 1983b.

Joseph, James A. "Six Trends Shaping Philanthropy's Future." *Foundation News*, May/June 1983c.

Joseph, James A. Testimony before the Sub-Committee on Commerce, Consumer, and Monetary Affairs, United States Congress, House of Representatives. Washington: May 11, 1983d.

Joseph, James A. "1969–1983: From Abuse to Access—A Different Spotlight." *Foundation News*, July/August 1983e.

Joseph, James A. "Professional Development: New Questions for a New Era." *Foundation News*, September/October 1983f.

Joseph, James A. "Why the Concern with Principles?" *Foundation News*, November/December 1983g.

Joseph, James A. "Private Versus Public Interest." *Foundation News*, January/February 1985a.

Joseph, James A. "When Foundations Seek to Shape Public Policy." *Foundation News*, March/April 1985b.

Joseph, James A. "Attracting and Retaining Talented People." *Foundation News*, May/June 1985c.

Joseph, James A. "Why Philanthropy: Provocative Answers." *Foundation News*, September/October 1985d.

Joseph, James A. "Why Philanthropy: The Civic Obligations of Community." *Foundation News*, November/December 1985e.

Joseph, James A. "Trusteeship in Transition." *Foundation News*, January/February 1986a.

Joseph, James A. "Philanthropy and Leadership." *Foundation News*, March/April 1986b.

Joseph, James A. "The Other Side of Professionalism." *Foundation News*, May/June 1986c.

Joseph, James A. "The Case for Corporate Giving." *Foundation News*, July/August 1986d.

Joseph, James A. "The Grantmaking Transaction." *Foundation News*, September/October 1986e.

Joseph, James A. "The Utopian Touch." *Foundation News*, November/December 1986f.

Josephs, Devereaux C. "President's Message." *Annual Report of the Carnegie Corporation.* New York: 1945.

Josephs, Devereaux C. "President's Message." *Annual Report of the Carnegie Corporation.* New York: 1947.

Karel, Frank. "Foundations and Public Policy: Coming of Age." *Foundation News,* March/April 1985.

Katz, Stanley N. "Report Card on the 'Nielsen Club.'" *Foundation News,* January/February 1986.

Kauffman, Joseph F. "Guiding the Fortunes of Academe." *Foundation News,* November/December 1986.

Keller, George. *Academic Strategy.* Baltimore: Johns Hopkins University, 1983.

Keller, George. "Trees Without Fruit." *Change,* January/February 1985.

Kennedy, Patrick. Editor's Note to "Guidelines on Grantmaking," by Lindsley F. Kimball. *Foundation News,* March/Arpil 1974.

Kennedy, Patrick. "An Interview with John May." *Foundation News,* September/October 1977.

Keppel, Frederick P. *The Foundation: Its Place in American Life.* New York: Macmillan and Company, 1930.

Keppel, Frederick P. *Philanthropy and Learning.* New York: Columbia University Press, 1936.

Keppel, Frederick P. "President's Message." *Annual Report of the Carnegie Corporation.* New York: 1939.

Kerlinger, Fred. *Foundations of Behavioral Research.* New York: Holt, Rinehart, and Winston, 1973.

Kiger, Joseph. *Operating Principles of the Larger Foundations.* New York: Russell Sage Foundation, 1954.

Kimball, Lindsley F. "Guidelines on Grantmaking." *Foundation News,* March/April 1974.

King, Cornelia S. *American Philanthropy: 1731 to 1860.* New York: Garland Publishing Company, 1984.

Kiritz, Norton J. "Proposal Checklist and Evaluation Form." *The Grantsmanship Center News,* July 1979.

Kirstein, George G. *Better Giving: The New Needs of American Philanthropy.* Boston: Houghton-Mifflin, 1975.

Knauft, E. B. "Looking into the Eighties." *Foundation News,* July/August 1980.

Knauft, E. B. "The End of Another Myth." *Foundation News,* September/October 1983.

Knauft, E. B. "The Filer Commission Revisited." *Foundation News,* January/February 1984.

Kramer, Martin. *The Venture Capital of Higher Education.* San Francisco: Jossey-Bass, 1980.

Kurzig, Carol. *Foundation Fundamentals: A Guide for Grantseekers.* New York: The Foundation Center, 1980 and 1986.

Kurzig, Carol. "The Foundation Center and Its Role in Research." In *New Directions for Institutional Advancement,* edited by J. David Ross. San Francisco: Jossey-Bass, November 1981.

Landau, Richard. "Do's and Don'ts for Development Officers." *Foundation News,* November/December 1975.

Laski, Harold J. "Foundations, Universities, and Research." *Harper's Monthly,* August 1928.

Laski, Harold J. *The Dangers of Obedience and Other Essays.* New York: Harper and Brothers, 1930.

Lefferts, Robert. *Getting a Grant in the 80s.* Englewood Cliffs, New Jersey, Prentice-Hall, 1982.

Lester, Robert. "The Philanthropic Endowment in Modern Life." *South Atlantic Quarterly,* January 1935.

Levy, Ferdinand and Gloria Shatto. "A Common Sense Approach to Corporate Giving." *Foundation News,* September/October 1979.

Lewis, Marianna, ed. *The Foundation Directory,* New York: The Foundation Center, 1971.

Light, Richard and David Pillemer. *Summing Up.* Cambridge, Massachusetts: Harvard University Press, 1984.

Lindeman, Eduard. *Wealth and Culture.* New York: Harcourt, Brace, and Company, 1936.

Lindeman, Eduard. "Wealth and Culture." In *Foundations Under Fire,* edited by Thomas Reeves. Ithaca, New York: Cornell University Press, 1970.

Lipscomb, James S. "Reproductive Rights: An Area of Foundation Concern?" *Foundation News,* July/August 1982.

Longenecker, Herbert E. "The Role of the Foundation Trustee." *The Philanthropy Monthly,* November 1974.

Lowry, W. McNeil. "Support for Humanities." In *Foundations: Twenty Viewpoints,* edited by F. Emerson Andrews. New York: Russell Sage Foundation, 1965.

Luttgens, Leslie. "Foundation Philanthropy: A New Era of Responsibility." *Foundation News,* September/October 1981.

Lyman, Richard W. "So You Want to Run a Foundation?" *Foundation News,* November/December 1982.

Macdonald, Dwight. *The Ford Foundation: The Men and the Millions.* New York: Reynal and Company, 1956.

Magarrell, Jack. "Less Money, More Competition for Grants Seen by Foundations." *The Chronicle of Higher Education,* November 3, 1980.

Magat, Richard. *The Ford Foundation at Work.* New York: Plenum Press, 1979.

Magat, Richard. "Decisions! Decisions!" *Foundation News,* March/April 1983a.

Magat, Richard. "Agreeing to Disagree." *Foundation News,* July/August 1983b.

Magat, Richard. "Out of the Shadows." *Foundation News,* July/August 1984.

Magat, Richard. "Mutual Nemesis: Foundations and Eduard Lindeman." *Foundation News,* May/June 1986.

Marchese, Theodore J., Alison Bernstein, and Frank Newman. "On the Foundations: What's the Issue." *Change,* January/February 1985.

Margolis, Richard J. "Moving America Right." *Foundation News,* July/August 1983.

Margolis, Richard J. " 'Small Wonders': The Perfect Fit." *Foundation News,* March/April 1985.

Marlowe, Howard. "What Foundations Should be Saying to Congress." *Foundation News,* November/December 1975.

Marquis, Samuel S. *Henry Ford: An Interpretation.* Boston: Little, Brown, 1923.

Marts, Arnaud. *Philanthropy's Role in Civilization.* New York: Harper and Brothers, 1953.

Marts, Arnaud. *The Generosity of Americans.* Englewood-Cliffs, New Jersey: Prentice-Hall, 1966.

Mauss, Marcel. *The Gift: Forms and Functions of Exchange in Archaic Societies.* London: Cohen and West, 1925.

Mayer, Richard A. "What Will a Foundation Look for When You Submit a Grant Proposal?" *Foundation Center Information Quarterly,* October 1972.

McCarthy, Kathleen D. *Noblesse Oblige: Charity and Cultural Philanthropy in Chicago.* University of Chicago Press: 1982.

McCarthy, Kathleen D. "Twenty-five Years and Change." *Foundation News,* November/December 1984.

McGuire, Betty E. "Plain English: The Language of Foundations." In *New Directions for Institutional Advancement,* edited by J. David Ross. San Francisco: Jossey-Bass, November 1981.

McIlnay, Dennis P. "Proposalese Spoken Here." *Currents.* July/August 1984.

McIlnay, Dennis P. "Proposalese." Paper presented at the annual meeting of the Council for the Advancement and Support of Education, New York, January 1985.

McMillen, Liz. "Corporate Gifts Called Investment, Not Impulse." *The Chronicle of Higher Education,* September 30, 1987a.

McMillen, Liz. "Foundations See No Short-Term Cutbacks from Big Losses, but Future is Uncertain." *The Chronicle of Higher Education,* October 28, 1987b.

McMillen, Liz. "Rockefeller Foundation Faces Continuing Questions About 'Vision,' but Has Gained Strength in 1980's." *The Chronicle of Higher Education,* January 27, 1988.

Menninger, Roy. "Foundation Work May be Hazardous to Your Health." New York: Council on Foundations, 1981.

Merrill, Charles. *The Checkbook: The Politics and Ethics of Foundation Philanthropy.* Boston: Oelgeschlager, Gunn, and Hain, 1986.

Miller, J. Irwin. "Time to Listen." *Foundation News,* May/June 1984.

Monroe, Helen. "We Must Maintain Integrity to Our Donors." *Foundation News,* May/June 1985.

Morison, Robert. "Foundations and Universities." *Daedalus,* Vol. 93, 1964.

Nason, John. *Trustees and the Future of Foundations.* New York: Council on Foundations, 1977.

National Center for Education Statistics. *The Condition of Education: 1983.* Washington: 1983.

National Center for Education Statistics. *Digest of Education Statistics: 1983–84*. Washington: 1984.

National Center for Education Statistics. *The Condition of Education: 1985*. Washington: 1985.

National Center for Education Statistics. *Financial Statistics of Institutions of Higher Education*. Washington, selected years.

National Committee for Responsive Philanthropy. *Philanthropy: Innovative and Important or Passive and Irrelevant?* Washington: 1977.

National Council of University Researchers. "Grant Making to Universities: A Proposal to Simplify Things." *Foundation News*, September/October 1974.

Nelson, Ralph L. "When More Is Less." *Foundation News*, March/April 1987.

Nevins, Allen. *John D. Rockefeller: A Study in Power*. New York: Charles Scribner and Sons, 1940.

Newton, Michael. Letter to Ben Whitaker, April 15, 1969.

Nielsen, Waldemar. "How Solid Are the Foundations?" *The New York Times*, October 21, 1962.

Nielsen, Waldemar. *The Big Foundations*. New York: Columbia University Press, 1972.

Nielsen, Waldemar. *The Endangered Sector*. New York: Columbia University Press, 1979.

Nielsen, Waldemar. "The Crisis of the Nonprofits." *Change*, January 1980.

Nielsen, Waldemar. *The Golden Donors*. New York: E. P. Dutton, 1985.

Nielsen, Waldemar. "How Golden Are the Golden Donors?" *Foundation News*, May/June 1986a.

Nielsen, Waldemar. "Double Crisis, Double Challenge." *Foundation News*, May/June 1986b.

Nietzsche, Friedrich. *Thus Spake Zarathustra*. Translated by Walter Kaufman. New York: Penguin Books, 1978.

O'Connell, Brian. "The Economic Recovery Program." *Foundation News*, March/April 1982.

O'Connell, Brian, ed. *America's Voluntary Spirit*. New York: The Foundation Center, 1983.

O'Connell, Brian. *The Board Member's Book*. New York: The Foundation Center, 1985.

Odendahl, Teresa and Elizabeth Boris. "A Delicate Balance: Board-Staff Relations." *Foundation News*, May/June 1983a.

Odendahl, Teresa and Elizabeth Boris. "The Grantmaking Process." *Foundation News*, September/October 1983b.

Odendahl, Teresa, Elizabeth Boris, and Arlene Daniels. *Working in Foundations*. New York: The Foundation Center, 1985.

Odendahl, Teresa and Catherine Sullivan. "America's Wealthy and the Future of Foundations." *Foundation News*, March/April 1986.

Odendahl, Teresa, ed. *America's Wealthy and The Future of Foundations*. New York: The Foundation Center, 1987.

Odendahl, Teresa. "Independent Foundations and Wealthy Donors: An Overview." In *America's Wealthy and the Future of Foundations*, edited by Teresa Odendahl. New York: The Foundation Center, 1987a.

Parrish, Thomas. "The Foundation: 'A Special American Institution,' " In *The Future of Foundations*, edited by Fritz Heimann. Englewood Cliffs, New Jersey: Prentice-Hall, 1973.

Patman, Wright. "The Free-Wheeling Foundations." *The Progressive*, June 1967.

Pattillo, Manning M. "Preparing the Foundation Proposal." In *Foundations: Twenty Viewpoints*, edited by F. Emerson Andrews. New York: Russell Sage Foundation, 1965.

Pattillo, Manning M. Speech to the annual conference of Southwest Foundations. Galveston, Texas: May 1969.

Patton, Michael Quinn. *Qualitative Evaluation Methods*. Beverly Hills, California: Sage Publications, 1980.

Payton, Robert. *Major Challenges to Philanthropy*. Washington: The Independent Sector, 1984.

Payton, Robert. "The Taming of the Corporation." *Change*, January/February 1985.

Peabody Education Fund. *Proceedings of the Trustees*. Boston, John Wilson and Son, 1875.

Penfield, Wilder. *The Difficult Art of Giving: The Epic of Alan Gregg*. Boston: Little, Brown, 1967.

Perkins, James A. "What the New Foundation Executive Should Know." In *Foundations: Twenty Viewpoints*, edited by F. Emerson Andrews. New York: Russell Sage Foundation, 1965.

Perry, Suzanne. "Getting a Foundation Grant Takes More than a Good Idea, Program Officers Say." *The Chronicle of Higher Education*. October 20, 1982.

Phelps, Edmund, ed. *Altruism, Morality, and Economic Theory*. New York: Russell Sage Foundation, 1975.

Philipp, Alicia. "Findings Should Not Be Shared." *Foundation News*, July/August 1983.

Phillips, E. Hereward. *Fundraising Techniques*. London: Basic Books, 1969.

Pierson, John. "A Little Focus Goes a Long Way." *Foundation News*, May/June 1982.

Pifer, Alan. "Legitimate and Essential: The Foundation Role in Public Policy." *Foundation News*, July/August 1975.

Pifer, Alan. *Philanthropy in an Age of Transition*. New York: The Foundation Center, 1984a.

Pifer, Alan. *Speaking Out*. Washington: Council on Foundations, 1984b.

Plinio, Alex. "Time for a Hard Look—At Ourselves." *Foundation News*, July/August 1986.

Pollard, John. *Fund Raising for Higher Education*. New York: Harper and Brothers, 1958.

Pritchett, Henry S. *A Comprehensive Plan of Insurance and Annuities for College Teachers*. New York: The Carnegie Foundation for the Advancement of Teaching, 1916.

Pritchett, Henry S. "A Science of Giving." *Annual Report of the Carnegie Corporation*. New York: 1922.

Pritchett, Henry S. "The Use and Abuse of Endowments." *Atlantic Monthly*, October 1929.

Public Relations Society. "The Changing Face of Philanthropy." *Public Relations Journal*, October 1984.

Quay, James K. "Experiences on Approaching Foundations." Paper presented at the conference on wills of the National Council of Churches of Christ. New York: 1952.

Radock, Michael. "The Fund Raising Role." Washington: Association of Governing Boards, February 1983.

Raffel, Burton. "A Critique of American Foundations." In *Foundations Under Fire*, edited by Thomas Reeves. Ithaca, New York: Cornell University Press, 1970.

Read, Patricia. Telephone conversation with author. December 29, 1986.

Reeves, Thomas, ed. *Foundations Under Fire*. Ithaca, New York: Cornell University Press, 1970.

Reeves, Thomas. "The Foundation and Freedoms." *Pacific Historical Review*, July 1974.

Reiss, Albert. "Whither the Craft?" *Sociological Inquiry*, Spring 1969.

Renz, Loren, ed. *The Foundation Directory*. New York: The Foundation Center, 1985.

Rich, Wilmer Shields. "Memorandum to the National Council on Community Foundations." September 5, 1962.

Richman, Saul. *Public Information Handbook for Foundations*. New York: Council on Foundations, 1973.

Richman, Saul. "Update on Annual Reports: Coming Out of the Stone Age." *Foundation News*, November/December 1975.

Richman, Saul. "Down the Highways and Byways with American Philanthropy." *Foundation News*, January/February 1980.

Rockefeller, David. "Foundation Fireside: Dusting the Mantel or Stirring the Ashes?" *Foundation News*, March/April 1973.

Rockefeller Foundation. *President's Five-Year Review and Annual Report*. New York: 1968.

Rockefeller, John D. "The Difficult Art of Giving." *The World's Work*, 1908.

Rockefeller, John D. *Random Reminiscences of Men and Events*. New York: 1909.

Rooks, Charles, ed. *The Grantmaking Process: Collection of Sample Materials*. Atlanta: Southeastern Council on Foundations, 1976.

Rosenwald, Julius. "Principles of Public Giving." *Atlantic Monthly*, May 1929.

Ross, J. David, ed. "Foundation Giving in Perspective." In *New Directions for Institutional Advancement*. San Francisco: Jossey-Bass, November 1981.

Rudney, Gabriel. "Creation of Foundations and Their Wealth." In *America's Wealthy and the Future of Foundations*, edited by Teresa Odendahl. New York: The Foundation Center, 1987.

Rudy, William H. *The Foundations: Their Use and Abuse*. Washington: Public Affairs Press, 1970.

Rusk, Dean. *The Role of the Foundation in American Life*. Claremont, California: Claremont University Press, 1961.

Russell, John. *Giving and Taking: Across the Foundation Desk*. New York: Columbia University Press, 1971.

Russell Sage Foundation. *Public Accountability of Foundations and Charitable Trusts*. New York: 1953.

Saario, Terry. "Sunshine, But Within Limits." *Foundation News*, July/August 1983.

Saasta, Timothy. "How Foundations Review Proposals and Make Grants." *The Grantsmanship Center News*, November 1976.

Salinger, Marion C. "In the Foundations." *The Chronicle of Higher Education*, May 4, 1983.

Scanlan, Joanne and Eugene. "Growing Fast." *Foundation News*, March/April 1986.

Schardt, Arlie. "Back to Congress—1983 Style." *Foundation News*, July/August 1983.

Schardt, Arlie. "To Be a Better Trustee." *Foundation News*, May/June 1984.

Schardt, Arlie. "Joining the Issues." *Foundation News*, May/June 1985.

Scriven, Michael. "Pros and Cons about Goal-Free Evaluation." *Evaluation Comment*, March 1972.

Seneca, Lucius Annaeus. *Moral Essays*. Cambridge, Massachusetts: Harvard University Press, 1964.

Seymour, Harold J. *Designs for Fund Raising*. New York: McGraw-Hill, 1966.

Shakespeare, William. *The Complete Works of William Shakespeare*. New York: Doubleday, 1946.

Sibley, Elbridge. *Support for Independent Scholarship and Research*. Washington: Social Science Research Council, 1951.

Simon, John. "Foundations and Public Controversy: An Affirmative View." In *The Future of Foundations*, edited by Fritz Heiman. Englewood Cliffs, New Jersey: Prentice-Hall, 1973.

Slater, John F. "Letter of Gift." May 4, 1882.

Sleeper, Jim. "The Foundations: Who, What, When, and How." *Change*, January/February 1985.

Smith, Kendrick. "Day of Judgment for a Fund Raiser." *Foundation News*, July/August 1979.

Somerville, Bill. "Bartering for a Grant is Repugnant." *Foundation News*, March/April 1983.

Spivack, Sydney S. "Foundations and Accountability." Master's thesis, Columbia University, 1953.

Springer, Cecile. "Dishonesty Has Never Been a Problem." *Foundation News*, January/February 1984.

Stamp, Tom. "Searching for Excellence." *Foundation News*, July/August 1987.

Stapleton, Darwin H. "Plumbing the Past." *Foundation News*, November/December 1987.

Stephens, Walter, ed. *Life and Writings of Turgot*. New York: Longmans, Green, and Company, 1895.

Stern, Philip M. "An Open Letter to the Ford Foundation." *Harper's*, January 1966.

Stevenson, J. John. "A Case Study: Lessons in Board Responsibility." *The Philanthropy Monthly*, October 1980.

Struckhoff, Eugene C. "Established Institutions, Foundations, and Change." *Foundation News,* January/February 1972.

Struckhoff, Eugene C. *The Handbook for Community Foundations.* New York: Council on Foundations, 1977.

Strunk, William and E. B. White. *The Elements of Style.* New York: The Macmillan Company, 1959.

Taft Group. *People in Philanthropy.* New York: 1986.

Teltsch, Kathleen. "Information Center Aids People Seeking a Grant." *The New York Times,* April 11, 1982.

Teltsch, Kathleen. "Streamlining the Ford Foundation." *The New York Times Magazine,* October 10, 1982.

Teltsch, Kathleen. "The Cousins: The Fourth Generation of Rockefellers." *The New York Times Magazine,* December 30, 1984.

Thaler, F. Roger. "What You Need to Know in Researching Foundations." In *New Directions for Institutional Advancement,* edited by J. David Ross. San Francisco: Jossey-Bass, November 1981.

Thibault, Edward A. "Alice in Moneyland." *Foundation News,* January/February 1973.

Thompkins, Bernard. "When You give—Are You Being Taken?" *Colliers,* June 25, 1954.

Thoreau, Henry David. "Economy." *Walden.* 1854.

Tivnan, Edward. "Foundations: A Time for Review." *The New York Times Magazine,* September 9, 1984.

Todd, A. J. "Mainsprings of Philanthropy." In *Intelligent Philanthropy,* edited by Ellsworth Faris. University of Chicago Press, 1930.

Townsend, Ted H. "Criteria Grantors Use in Assessing Proposals." *Foundation News,* March/April 1974.

United States Congress. *Congressional Record.* January 22, 1962.

United States House of Representatives. *Answers to Questionnaire.* Select Committee to Investigate Foundations and Other Charitable Organizations, Washington: 1952a.

United States House of Representatives. *Letters from Various Individuals.* Select Committee to Investigate Foundations and Other Charitable Organizations, Washington: 1952b.

United States House of Representatives. *Final Report of the Select Committee to Investigate Foundations and Other Charitable Organizations,* Washington: 1952c.

United States Treasury Department. *Report on Private Foundations.* February 1965.

Urrows, Henry and Elizabeth. "TRA '69: Coming Up on Ten Years." *Foundation News,* May/June 1979.

Urrows, Henry and Elizabeth. "John Simon: An Interview." *Foundation News,* July/August 1981.

Vanguard Public Foundation. *Robin Hood Was Right: Giving Your Money for Social Change.* San Francisco: 1977.

Veblen, Thorstein. *The Theory of the Leisure Class.* New York: Modern Library, 1931.

Viscusi, Margo. "Annual Reports: Making a Good Idea Better." *Foundation News*, January/February 1985a.

Viscusi, Margo. "Coming of Age." *Foundation News*, May/June 1985b.

Wadsworth, Homer C. "The Role of the Foundation in Community Affairs." In *Foundations: Twenty Viewpoints*, edited by F. Emerson Andrews. New York: Russell Sage Foundation, 1965.

Wall, Joseph Frazier. *Andrew Carnegie*. Oxford University Press, 1970.

Warm, Harriet. "How Grantseekers Lower the Odds." *Foundation News*, July/August 1979.

Washington, Booker T. *Up from Slavery: An Autobiography*. New York: Doubleday and Company, 1963.

Weaver, Warren. "Thought on Philanthropy and Philanthropoids." In *Foundations: Twenty Viewpoints*, edited by F. Emerson Andrews. New York: Russell Sage Foundation, 1965.

Weaver, Warren. *U.S. Philanthropic Foundations*. New York: Harper and Row, 1967.

Weaver, Warren. *Scene of Change*. New York: Charles Scribner and Sons, 1970.

Weischadle, David E. "Carnegie: A Case Study in How Foundations Make Decisions." *Phi Delta Kappa*, October 1977.

West, Herbert B. "The Art of Giving Money Away." *Foundation News*, September/October 1968.

Whitaker, Ben. *The Philanthropoids*. Birkenhead, England: Eyre Methuen Ltd., 1874.

Whiting, Basil J. "Is There a New Grantor-Grantee Relationship?" *Foundation News*, November/December 1973.

Wilbur, Colburn. "Write-Ups Are Private." *Foundation News*, July/August 1983.

Willey, M. and Dale Patterson. "Philanthropic Endowments and Their Grants to Higher Education During the Depression Years." *School and Society*, May 8, 1937.

Williams, Roger M. "An Interview with William E. Simon." *Foundation News*, September/October 1983.

Williams, Roger M. "The Readiest Reference." *Foundation News*, November/December 1984.

Williams, Roger M. "Gulling the Grantseeker." *Foundation News*, July/August 1985.

Wormser, Rene A. *Foundations: Their Power and Influence*. New York: Devin-Adair, 1968.

Yankelovich, Daniel. "Dramatic Changes in the 80s." *Foundation News*, July/August 1982.

Yarmolinsky, Adam. "The Foundation as an Expression of a Democratic Society." *Proceedings of the Fifth Biennial Conference on Charitable Foundations*. Albany, New York: Bender and Company, 1961.

Young, Donald. "Support for Social Research." In *Foundations: Twenty Viewpoints*, edited by F. Emerson Andrews. New York: Russell Sage Foundation, 1965.

Young, Donald. "Support for Social Research." In *Foundations Under Fire*, edited by Thomas Reeves. Ithaca, New York: Cornell University Press, 1970.

Young, Donald and Wilbert Moore. *Trusteeship and the Management of Foundations*. New York: Russell Sage Foundation, 1969.

Young, James. "Dead Hand in Philanthropy." *Current History*, March 1926.

Zinsser, Hans. "The Perils of Magnanimity: A Problem in American Education." *Atlantic Monthly*, February 1927.

Zurcher, Arnold J. *The Management of American Foundations*. New York University Press, 1972.

Zurcher, Arnold J. and Jane Dustan. *The Foundation Administrator*. New York: Russell Sage Foundation, 1972.

INDEX

181